THE FATEFUL
ENDS AND SHADES
OF SALT

Ridgway

Please
Return to: General M. B. Ridgway
918 W. Waldheim Road
Pittsburgh, Pa. 15215

NATIONAL STRATEGY INFORMATION CENTER, INC.

x NSIC

THE FATEFUL ENDS AND SHADES OF SALT

Past ... Present ... And Yet To Come?

Paul H. Nitze
James E. Dougherty
and
Francis X. Kane

PUBLISHED BY

CRANE, RUSSAK & COMPANY, INC.
NEW YORK

The Fateful Ends and Shades of SALT:
Past . . . Present . . . And Yet to Come?

Published in the United States by
Crane, Russak & Company, Inc.
3 East 44th Street
New York, New York 10017

Copyright © *1979 by* National Strategy Information Center, Inc.
111 East 58th Street
New York, New York 10022

ISBN   0-8448-1332-X
LC   78-78392

Printed in the United States of America

Table of Contents

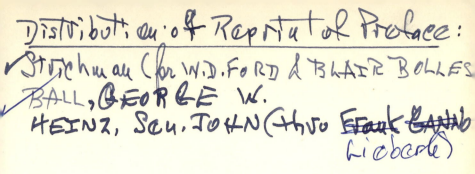

PREFACE

Those who voice dismay over Israeli and Egyptian inability to transmute the good intentions of Camp David into lasting agreements in ninety days might reflect that America and Russia have been negotiating SALT II for more than six years. When the preservation of the national entity is at stake, the facile imagery of peace-seeking should yield to the sobering need for realistic audits of fateful military trade-offs. No wonder, then, if the Israeli Parliament had second thoughts about giving up Sinai oil fields and air bases for Cairo's hedged promises, or the U.S. Congress proves skeptical of White House reliance on a Brezhnev letter of "no evil intent" to restrict the range and targets of Backfire bombers. No wonder either if Congress will enquire why the Carter/Vance version of arms "control" could leave the Soviets with a 6-1 edge in counterforce capability.

In some not too distant crisis, both U.S. will and the morale of our allies can be enervated by Russia's nuclear preponderance. Strategic imbalance creates a vector for the levers of diplomacy or armored divisions; and, in the cold twilight of SALT II, overawed Western politicians may feel compelled to allow Soviet naval squadrons and airborne armies to move, unopposed, to cement Moscow's dominion of the Middle East.

If SALT II compounds the trend towards inferiority

vii

which the U.S. unwisely accepted at SALT I, why not call the whole thing off? Why pretend that sounding brass is the durable, intricate key to peace? Neither the peril to our cities nor military budgets nor Communist ambitions have been attenuated by SALT. The incentive to strike first in a moment of political tension is enhanced, as is the premium for acquiring "laser deathrays" and other deadly novelties not covered by the Treaty. When illusions are put aside, it will be seen that the chief consequence of interminable arms talks between the superpowers has been to afford the Russians more than a decade to neutralize America's once formidable lead in weapons technology.

How then can we explicate the curious passion to persist in the losing gamble of SALT? The simplistic answer that "without SALT a return to the arms race may impose an intolerable cost" will not bear scrutiny. The Russians are already on the near edge of mobilization for war, spending 40% more than we do for arms, from a GNP roughly half our own. In brief, Moscow is near to her weapons peak right now, while we have been resting on a lower plateau. But for not more than an added 1.5% of the GNP for U.S. defense—a percentage less than we spent in Eisenhower's day—we could procure the means to shield the nation from a first strike, a more important goal than inducing Brezhnev to initial more paper.

To some in the Arms Control and Disarmament Agency (ACDA) and the Department of State, however, it seems "unthinkable" to repudiate SALT even if that act would free our aerospace industry, at bearable cost, to repair the ominous leaks in our security umbrella. Perhaps for not a few American officials an arms treaty with the Russians is akin to the Bridge over the River K'wai; not conceiving what dread traffic it may encourage, they build it "simply because they are there" and an onerous task calls forth their skill in precision design. (Of course, a society which extends fame and political rewards to leaders who build bad treaties, rather than urge no treaty at all, is itself a culpable actor in the national psychodrama of bridging the K'wai or, in this case, drowning in SALT.)

The Senate debate over ratification of the Treaty promises to be as strenuous as it is imperative. If war is too serious to be left to the generals, throw-weight inferiority is too critical to be casually embraced by our diplomats; and Senators can help the rest of us to sort out the hazards in the ambiguity of "essential equivalence." Certainly the issues are more technical and arcane than in the case of the battle over the Panama Canal; and one hopes that wellworn polemics about "overkill" will yield to a more measured assessment of the "accuracy revolution" and what that may entail for the outmoded premise of mutual assured destruction (MAD). If the rationale for a MAD strategy of averting war was ever valid, it is less than compelling in an era when both sides can perfect counterforce capabilities through precision-guidance.

In debating the new treaty, we should remember that, although SALT I stultified America's substantial lead in ABM technology, it did little else to effectively curb arms competition. Paradoxically, it stimulated the drive to upgrade weapons by placing an innocuous limit to a "stockpile race" of earlier generation missiles while, at the same time, offering irresistible incentives to the winners of the "R&D race" for superiority in the art of blinding or destroying enemy systems before they can do their job. Inescapably, this imposes on the U.S. side (sievelike with respect to state secrets) a vastly unequal task of verification. To police SALT I, one needed a manageable count of relatively easy to find launch vehicles. To verify the complex calculus of "essential equivalence," derived from the much more intricate arms restraints attempted by SALT II, may well require an almost theological disbelief in Soviet duplicity as well as the combined (yet still inadequate?) electronic resources of the CIA, Defense Intelligence Agency, and National Security Agency.

One also expects that Senators, unlike Brahmins in ACDA and the Department of State, will not be over-zealous to subordinate U.S. strategy to the canons of SALT II by discounting in advance our latent techno-logical advantages. Security, not SALT, is the primary aim; while disarmament may or may not be an appro-priate means, especially if equity is camouflaged and traded away. Why, for example, budget 3% more for NATO's defense at the conventional level, if a bad SALT—by failing to balance Soviet SS-20s with effective Ground-Launched Cruise Missiles in West Germany—is perceived by our allies to *diminish* NATO's shield by 10%?

Arms treaties with Moscow have been repeatedly oversold—by both Republican and Democratic Adminis-trations—as the touchstone of good relations between the superpowers. We are promised, if SALT succeeds, a generation of peace; if it fails, we are threatened with a return to the Cold War and a ruinous arms race. The Soviets know better; with or without SALT, they wage a one-sided war (both cold and hot—especially in Asia and Africa) and run a unilateral arms race. Therefore, let us not again accept a bad treaty on the threadbare illu-sion that it will enmesh the Russians in Judeo-Christian mores; for SALT is neither the centerpiece of detente, nor the single scale in which the military balance is weighed. Moscow has always regarded SALT as a *campaign* rather than an objective.

The Politburo utilizes arms talks—as it battens on Western credits and technology transfers—as part of its grand design to further alter the correlation of forces in its favor. Thus, both America's safety and the security of NATO-Europe, Japan, and the Middle East depend on SALT II's deterrent effect. The Senate and the American public should not be beguiled by spurious arguments that even a flawed SALT will shore up the credibility of the Presidency, or improve Soviet behavior in Africa, or pave the way for some future SALT-in-the-sky when a benign Politburo may generously annul all the cumulative military advantages we have given them in SALT I and SALT II. Given the "window of opportunity" which opens for the Soviet war-machine in the time frame 1982-86, this may be the last U.S. SALT debate which is "uncoerced" by adversary military arsenals beyond our power to contest. It may also be our last, 11th hour opportunity to redress the adverse military balance by more generous cooperation with the defense communities of West Europe and Japan—especially in unrestricted Cruise missile technology—even if that means a postponement or rejection of SALT II. Far better to disappoint the Russians than to generate despondency among allies.

If comparative numbers of launchers and sizes of payloads alone determined the strategic balance, it would be relatively easy to form a judgment as to whether SALT II provides "essential equivalence." (Even then, not too easy. If the crocodile agrees to use only half the force of his armored tail on land, does a swimming tiger renounce front teeth or rear claw?) But more complex questions must be addressed—e.g.: (1) Comparatively, how *vulnerable* are silos and how *accurate,* warheads? (2) Could some launchers be reloaded by a Party determined to cheat? (3) Does apparent parity in overall numbers disguise a hidden threat from Soviet "heavy" missiles (a type we lack)? (4) Will "crisis stability" and alliance cohesion be enhanced or undermined by gray area systems? (5) What is the projected state of the art in anti-submarine warfare (plus ABM research, permitted by SALT I), and how will those technologies affect "assured deterrence" from the seas? (6) Is the alert status of U.S. bombers sufficient to protect them from a surprise strike from Soviet SLBMs? (7) How secure are space reconnaissance vehicles against laser-blinding and killer-satellites? (8) Is the "survivability" of the Command, Control, and Communications system of an open America dangerously inferior to that of a closed Russia? (9) How is strategic parity affected by terminal guidance for ICBMs, hardening of silos, city evacuation drills, and forward bases for submarines? (10) Might SALT II's formulae drive us to the extremity of a "launch on warning" reflex? (11) How, truly, is "equity" achieved between two superpowers with different geographies, strategies, import/export needs, commitments to allies, and political goals? (12) Are the present means of verifying the Treaty equal in sophistication to the burgeoning technologies of missile mobility, cold launch release, and "interchangeability" (i.e.—adding a third stage to the Soviet SS-20 to convert it into an intercontinental SS-16)?

Not only weapons but military doctrines must be taken into account in trying to evaluate "operational parity." Here the "culture gap" is perhaps wider than the missile gap, for in Soviet military literature nuclear war is quite thinkable. Indeed "weapons of mass destruction" are regarded as so inevitable a part of the future battlefield that a great deal of Red Army training is based on that assumption. Consider the implications of the following divergence in concept and doctrine:

U.S.		USSR
deterrence	vs.	war-fighting; war-winning
retaliation	vs.	pre-emption; shock and surprise
mutual assured destruction	vs.	post-attack recovery
"the living will envy the dead"	vs.	*national entity survival!*

The Soviets have always rejected our postulate that nuclear war would necessarily lead to mutual suicide; hence, their refusal to emulate the U.S. in virtually abandoning air defense and civil defense. Moscow seems to comprehend that one of the "two scorpions in a bottle" may escape an inevitable common fate when, in the early 1980s, perhaps no more than one-third of the Soviet MIRVed missile force could destroy 90% of our Minutemen silos, most of our bombers, and that portion of our submarine fleet in port. True, we could still mount a retaliatory strike from the remnants of our Poseidon and Trident fleets, but the warheads on SLBMs are smaller and less accurate than their land-based cousins. (A mere 25 of the 300-plus Soviet "heavy" SS-18 missiles carry more megatons than our entire submarine fleet; so it is scarcely a "balance" of terror when an American President, in order to kill 25 million Russians in a second strike, would risk losing 100 million of his countrymen to a Soviet third strike.)

A Soviet pre-emptive strike against our bombers and larger missiles, coordinated with vigorous air and civil defense preparations, might tempt the Politburo to feel it could assure the survival of the governing Communist elites, a creative corps of scientists and managers, plus the necessary cadres of engineers and technicians to re-build the USSR within a decade. Thus, political asymmetries could be almost as distorting as throw-weight imbalance: e.g., (1) in the U.S., it is thought impolitic even to protect Congress, the Pentagon, and the White House with an ABM system around Washington, D.C.; but (2) in the USSR, the continuance of the Communist command structure, not the survival of the Soviet peoples as a whole, might well constitute the essence of "national value preservation." Given dispersal of indus-try throughout the enormous land mass of the Soviet continent, more than 12,000 SAMs guarding the heart-land, continuing research on anti-ballistic missile de-fense, and the opportunity to evacuate elites before launching a surprise attack, guaranteeing the survival of the Communist control apparatus is by no means an "unthinkable" task for a totalitarian oligarchy. The military implications of SALT II, therefore, or the plausibility of worst case scenarios, cannot be rationally rejected by a culture-blind appeal to the humanistic values and democratic ethic of American society.

It may seem oddly biased for critics to object to another dose of SALT from Messrs. Carter and Vance when the nation swallowed the SALT of Messrs. Nixon and Kissinger, the masters of *realpolitik*. Surely, if anti-Communist Republicans conceded a 40% edge to the Soviets in ICBM launchers and a 34% edge in SLBMs, why can't Democrats yield a bit on throw-weight and the Backfire or accept a few restrictions on the range of Cruise missiles? (Although SALT I was hailed as "braking Soviet momentum," perhaps the best thing one can say for the lapsed Treaty is that: "Brought forth in the vortex of anti-war sentiment over Vietnam, it helped calm the campus but proved a failed experiment in curtailing the Soviet drive for superiority.")

Unhappily for the principle of bipartisan "fairness," you can't step in the same saltwater twice. The U.S., in 1972, gave Russia the best of the SALT I bargain from our platform of what seemed at the time to be unassailable superiority in bombers, MIRV technology, accuracy and number of warheads, and forward bases (hence more time on station) for America submarines. Today, nearly seven years later, the military-geopolitical matrix has changed; we have no more margin for error; we are even behind in some categories of weaponry and (at best) in a posture of parity on others. SALT II takes place not in the context of overall American superiority, some portions of which can be safely diminished, but at a time when Washington can no longer afford to write-off dubious "tests" of Soviet good intentions. All things human are forever in flux, and U.S. military power in the SALT II era, like the 1979 American dollar, has lost some of its former potency. Our missiles and our money have both been devalued in comparison with other forces and currencies in the world arena. Hence our traditional generosity to adversaries at the negotiating table ought to be modified by awareness of our vulnerabilities in a new set of bleaker circumstances.

Further, the nation can profit if the Senate debate over SALT II is expanded to encompass the relation of strategic nuclear umbrellas to the viability of theater forces in West Europe and the Middle East, the vulnerability and morale of allies, and conventional arms balances. With or without SALT II, our ICBMs can be scotched in their nests by, say, 1982; and, quite apart from that Treaty, power will continue to shift away from us if Washington persists in unilateral (and unrequited) steps towards disarmament. It is relevant, even imperative, to re-examine the decision to cancel or delay such weapons as the B-1 bomber, the MX missile, and enhanced radiation warheads. Nor is it beside the point to assess the prospects for peace in a near-term future in which the Soviets have parity-plus in strategic weapons but also outproduce us 7-1 in tanks and 5-1 in artillery.

In a well-orchestrated strategy (which we lack), the whole can sometimes equal the multiplication of its parts. Thus, a Soviet advantage derived from SALT is not merely a trump at the nuclear level; it can be used to "pin down" NATO and "transfix" Washington while Moscow mounts aggression on wholly diverse fronts. Consider the "linkage" that may matter most—and is seldom broached—between (1) the SS-18s targeted on our heartland; (2) the SS-20s (aimed at Europe, unlimited by SALT), whose massive potential could paralyze NATO into futile handwringing in some future Mid-East crisis; and (3) Soviet Backfires providing undisputed air superiority for coups or insurgencies directed at Saudi Arabia or another Arab war against Israel. SALT II cannot, in logic or prudence, be separated from a discussion of comparative strategy, gray area systems, the undeclared "resource war" waged by Russia and Cuba in Africa, the crippling loss of our intelligence window in Iran, or the likely psychological impact of a post-SALT II euphoria on American willingness to cope in other dimensions with a USSR spending (in 1978) up to $40 billion more than we are on armament. Of course some forms of linkage -- especially between diplomacy and weaponry -- might eventuate in "security whiplash."

If the Russians promise to keep Cubans out of Rhodesia, does "linkage" imply we should not then require Moscow to keep Backfires out of range of American cities? We should be wary of linking ratification of SALT restrictions—that would "lock-up" U.S. technology for five years—to Soviet "good behavior" in the Third World that might last barely six months and is, in any case, unilaterally reversible outside the provisions of the Treaty.

Inasmuch as part of the impetus for signing SALT I came from Henry Kissinger's profound pessimism that the American people—in the wake of Vietnam—were not prepared for sacrifice in support of national power, this time the debate over SALT II ought to put that theory to the test by giving the public enough data and analysis to make a conscious choice. This brings us to our reason for publishing *The Fateful Ends and Shades of SALT: Past...Present...And Yet to Come?* It is the hope of the National Strategy Information Center that the three essays contained herein will contribute usefully to this debate.

Our first author, James E. Dougherty, in his article entitled "SALT: An Introduction to the Substance and Politics of the Negotiations," examines the larger political framework in which U.S.-Soviet arms negotiations are being conducted. Dr. Dougherty provides a review of the SALT I accords, the Vladivostok Agreement, the Carter Proposal of March 1977 and its rejection by the Soviets, and the provisions of the tentative SALT II agreement, focusing on those issues which have made agreement between the superpowers so difficult and elusive.

In "The Merits and Demerits of a SALT II Agreement," the Honorable Paul H. Nitze details the likely effects of the proposed accords on the various components of the U.S.-Soviet military balance and analyzes the probable impact of the agreement on the ability of the U.S. to reverse adverse trends. In Mr. Nitze's view, the SALT II agreement has sacrificed important American arms control and security objectives, and he argues that "U.S. program decisions and delays in making decisions since Vladivostok, combined with the terms of the probable SALT II agreement, now make it difficult, if not impossible, for the U.S. to maintain crisis stability and rough equivalence."

In the final essay, entitled "Safeguards from SALT: U.S. Technological Strategy in an Era of Arms Control," Francis X. Kane focuses on the technological climate the U.S. will face in coming decades. Dr. Kane argues that to ensure U.S. security the SALT II accords must be accompanied by a program of weapon systems development and acquisition which can provide "safeguards" against deficiencies in the accords and against the possibility of treaty failure or abrogation. The implementation of innovative research and development programs is essential, in his view, for such measures will enable the U.S. to respond without panic and the resulting high cost solutions if Soviet breakaway programs threaten U.S. interests. Kane further shows how prudent arms control measures combined with an effective technological strategy can lead to the achievement of two basic U.S. objectives—the maintenance of a stable balance of strategic power and the negotiation of mutual reductions in the level of strategic forces.

Dr. James E. Dougherty is Professor of Political Science and former Executive Vice President, Saint Joseph's University, Philadelphia. He is also Senior Staff Member of the Institute for Foreign Policy Analysis, Cambridge, Massachusetts. He is author of *Arms Control and Disarmament: The Critical Issues* (1966) and *How to Think About Arms Control and Disarmament* (1973). In addition to other books, Dr. Dougherty has also contributed numerous articles on arms control and disarmament matters to *Orbis, Current History, The New Catholic Encyclopaedia,* and other publications.

The Honorable Paul H. Nitze served as the representative of the Secretary of Defense to the United States Delegation to the SALT negotiations from the Spring of 1969 through June 1974. Prior to this appointment, he served as Deputy Secretary of Defense (1967-1969), Secretary of the Navy (1963-1967), and Assistant Secretary of Defense, International Security Affairs (1961-1963). Mr. Nitze is Chairman of the Advisory Council of The Johns Hopkins School of Advanced International Studies in Washington, D.C., and is Director of Policy Studies for The Committee on the Present Danger.

Dr. Francis X. Kane is a member of the Professional Staff of TRW Defense and Space Systems Group, Redondo Beach, California. He has spent over thirty-five years as a planner of future systems and technology, principally in the areas of space and ballistic missiles; his present area of work focuses on the impact of SALT on future strategic systems, such as the MX ICBM. Dr. Kane graduated from the U.S. Military Academy and earned his Ph.D. from Georgetown University. He has taught at the Graduate School of Catholic University, Pepperdine College, and the University of California at Los Angeles, and has published articles in a number of journals.

The National Strategy Information Center extends its special appreciation to The Committee on the Present Danger for permission to publish in this Agenda Paper major portions of a paper by Mr. Nitze originally distributed under the auspices of the Committee.

Frank R. Barnett, *President*
National Strategy Information Center

March 1979

1

SALT: An Introduction to the Substance and Politics of the Negotiations

James E. Dougherty

For considerably more than a year now, highly placed policy-makers in Washington have been saying that the United States and the Soviet Union have moved about 90 percent of the way toward the conclusion of a Strategic Arms Limitation Talks (SALT) II agreement limiting strategic weapons. Apparently the achievement of the last 10 percent has been extremely difficult and elusive. As the year 1979 began, the probability that there would be a SALT II agreement in the near future appeared somewhat better than fifty-fifty.

THE CURRENT CONDITION OF DETENTE

Both the United States and the Soviet Union recognize that there are formidable difficulties standing in the way of a final SALT II Treaty. Some of these difficulties, of course, inhere in every effort to regulate the distribution of military power between two major political-ideological rivals, each of which naturally prefers to impose limits on the other and preserve maximum freedom for itself. Some arise out of the futility of trying to employ the unchanging language of diplomatic-legalistic documents to establish fairly durable controls over a rapidly changing military technology. In the present context, some of the difficulties are also attributable to a more or less steady deterioration in U.S.-Soviet political relations since early 1977.

This deterioration is not easy to explain. In fact, it contains several anomalies. Detente seemed to be at its zenith in 1972, when the SALT I Accords were signed, even though the Vietnam War was still going on; and there was still something left to the Washington-Moscow "spirit of detente" after the brief superpower confrontation at the time of the Middle East crisis in October 1973. Under President Jimmy Carter, the United States has not been involved in any "foreign imperialist wars"; it has generally been perceived as shifting toward a somewhat more neutral posture with respect to the Arab-Israeli conflict; and instead of initiating the deployment of new weapons systems (as President Nixon and Secretary of State Kissinger were disposed to do in the case of Safeguard Anti-Ballistic Missiles [ABM]) as a bargaining chip for arms negotiations, the Carter Administration, while talking a great deal about new weapons, has either unilaterally cancelled them (the B-1 bomber), deferred the decision to develop them (the neutron bomb), or entered into SALT negotiations about them before development begins (the MX mobile missile) or while they are still in the early stages of development and testing (Cruise missiles). Because the SALT II negotiations have dragged on until they are now in their seventh year, however, it has become necessary for the Carter Administration to give serious consideration to new programs of strategic weapons modernization. This has further complicated the effort to reach agreement, as will be discussed below.

The deterioration of the Soviet-American detente has usually been attributed to the following factors: 1) President Carter's human rights campaign, despite the President's frequent assertions that it is universal, not aimed specifically at the Soviet Union, and need not affect

SALT negotiations; 2) Soviet-Cuban activity in Africa, especially in the Horn, and the unfavorable U.S. reaction to it, despite the warning of some North Atlantic Treaty Organization (NATO) allies not to overreact; 3) a growing apprehensiveness among defense-knowledgeable elites in the United States and Western Europe over the steady Soviet buildup of strategic (i. e., anti-U.S.) capabilities and European theater capabilities (both nuclear and conventional); 4) Soviet frustration at not being able to import all desired technology from the West and at having unacceptable conditions imposed upon Soviet-U.S. trade; 5) Soviet irritation at being excluded from Middle East negotiations; 6) the failure of the Soviets to reciprocate unilateral U.S. arms restraint policies; and 7) the recent tendency of the United States to play the "China card," culminating in the visit of Deputy Prime Minister Teng Hsiao-Ping in early 1979.

It should be noted that most of the foregoing concerns antedate the Carter Administration. There had been a Ford-Kissinger warning about Soviet-Cuban activity in Africa. The United States did not seem able to do much about it then, and its political capability in this respect has not substantially improved, but the non-aligned nations, meeting at Belgrade in July 1978, hinted for the first time that they are becoming more worried about Soviet expansionism than about Western imperialism.[1] American and European policymakers have been worried for at least a decade, since the invasion of Czechoslovakia, about the European theater balance, and since 1970 about the deployment of Soviet "heavy" strategic missiles. Congress had linked U.S. trade credits to Soviet Jewish emigration two years before Carter was elected, and Moscow had been chagrined since early 1974 at being left out of U.S. peace diplomacy in the Middle East. The new elements in the situation are the failure of the Soviets to reciprocate Carter's unusual unilateral arms restraint policies (which is really not surprising to anyone acquainted with the Soviets' penchant for hard bargaining) and President Carter's human rights campaign. A partly old, partly new element is the U.S. policy toward China. Before turning to the SALT II Treaty itself and its prospect for Senate ratification, something should be said about Soviet activity in Africa, the human rights issue, and the American China policy as parts of the larger political framework in which U.S.-Soviet arms negotiations are being conducted.

Soviet-Cuban military adventures in Africa complicated the SALT II negotiations in the Spring of 1978. Ambiguous signals issued from Secretary of State Cyrus R. Vance, National Security Adviser Zbigniew Brzezinski, and President Carter himself on whether there was any direct connection between Soviet meddling in the Horn of Africa and the slowing of progress in SALT. Regardless of official U.S. denials of a formal linkage, the Soviets cannot but realize that in the Senate ratification debate a connection would probably be drawn between SALT and developments in the larger framework of global diplomacy and strategy. In May 1978 the NATO heads of government, meeting in Washington, warned Moscow that Soviet and Cuban military activity in Africa would "jeopardize the further improvement of East-West relations."[2]

A few weeks later, *Pravda* declared that "changes dangerous to the cause of peace are taking place" in U.S. policy. The Communist organ accused the United States, or groups within it, of trying to undermine detente and return the world to the Cold War; bring about a deliberate worsening of bilateral relations with the U.S.S.R.; interfere in Soviet internal affairs; and find a "common language with the aggressive anti-Sovietism of the Chinese rulers."[3] The last reference was a jibe directed against the May visit to Peking by Brzezinski, who in the eyes of Soviet leaders harbors a deep-rooted emotional hostility against them because of his East European background. Despite their vast military superiority vis-a-vis China, the Soviets react with great sensitivity to any diplomatic tilt toward China by the United States. The Nixon-Kissinger "opening to Peking" was dangerous enough in Soviet eyes, but the frightening aspects of that maneuver had been attenuated by two facts: 1) it had a largely symbolic-ceremonial character and, although it introduced a new uncertainty into Soviet calculations, it produced no clear change in the world power balance; and 2) it was accompanied by an intensification of efforts to advance the Soviet-American detente, culminating in SALT I and the U.S. military withdrawal from Southeast Asia. In contrast, the Carter-Brzezinski policy toward the Peking regime has taken shape at a time of worsening U.S.-Soviet relations and might appear to be aimed at the technological buildup of China, with the trade cooperation of Western Europe, Japan, and the United States.[4]

The Carter Administration has taken the position that a closer U.S.-China relationship is inevitable and need not cause undue concern in Moscow. It has also given assurances that U.S. technology transfers will not include arms. Soviet leaders, however, worry about any kind of technological development in China. They blame Washington for doing nothing to discourage French sales of antitank and antiaircraft missiles or British sales of Harrier jet fighters and diesel engines for coast guard craft. Apparently unimpressed by Western distinctions between offensive and defensive arms, Soviet leaders have insinuated that President Carter has tried to use the U.S.-China relation as an anti-Soviet lever. At the same time they have denied that the Carter decision of December 1978 to grant full diplomatic recognition to the People's Republic of China lessened their interest in concluding SALT II, or motivated any delay on their side. Some observers wondered whether the Soviets' warnings that the Western allies, in their new approach to China, might be "playing with fire" reflected an historic paranoid suspicion of the whole outside world and an apprehensiveness that the Chinese, the Germans, the Japanese, and the Americans (all the peoples they fear the most) might be in the process of coalescing against them. Others thought that the Soviet leaders might merely wish to assess fully the significance of the Teng visit to Washington before finally agreeing to a SALT II Treaty. Meanwhile, Washington was not able entirely to dismiss the possibility that in a delicate triangular relationship Moscow and Peking might decide to play their own card of Sino-Soviet rapprochement.[5]

The trials of Anatoli Shcharansky, Viktoras Pektus, and Alexander Ginzburg in July 1978 sent further storm clouds into the atmosphere of Soviet-American relations. The Shcharansky trial in particular, in view of Soviet charges concerning a CIA connection in contradiction to Carter's statements, was widely portrayed as a calculated affront to the President. One British journal called the trial "a highly dangerous flashpoint for U.S.-Soviet relations."[6]

International political rhetoric escalated toward a new hostility in 1978. The tension was exacerbated by an increasing tendency on the part of the Soviets to mete out severe treatment to American journalists, businessmen, and diplomats, and also by President Carter's decision to cancel the sale of computers and oil-drilling equipment, as well as to curtail the exchange of scientific commissions and high-level governmental officials. There was the possibility that each side was merely trying to demonstrate the firmness of its determination[7] before entering into a SALT II agreement which, if ever concluded, would surely be subjected to severe criticism by the tougher-minded persons in each country—publicly in the United States, behind closed doors in the Kremlin.

Perhaps President Carter's apparently tough stance on human rights, his call for increased defense spending to strengthen NATO readiness, and his proposal for stepped-up U.S. civil defense preparations may have been calculated primarily to win over some domestic critics of SALT II. If this were to prove to be the case, the signing of a SALT II Treaty might well lead to a rapid thaw in U.S.-Soviet relations—a thaw which would, in the thinking of some of those critics, tempt the President to embark upon a different course and to assign a lower priority to those defense needs that the Administration was emphasizing prior to the conclusion of a SALT II agreement. Perhaps the "little Cold War" was nothing more than stage-talk.

THE QUESTION OF SENATE RATIFICATION

When the Senate approved the Interim Agreement on Offensive Strategic Weapons in September 1972, it expressed concern over the numerical superiority assigned to the U.S.S.R. The Senate adopted the Jackson Amendment stipulating that any future U.S.-Soviet treaty must not codify U.S. inferiority. (This will be discussed more fully below in the section "From SALT I to SALT II.") Many Senators have become genuinely alarmed by the Soviet strategic buildup of recent years. The Soviets have blamed the Congress for the slow pace of the SALT negotiations, and have warned the Carter Administration against trying to use the threat of Senate rejection to obtain concessions from Moscow.[8]

By the spring of 1978 the Carter Administration, which had just made a herculean effort to win a narrow victory on the Panama Canal Treaties, realized that it faced a much stiffer battle on SALT.[9] A number of Senators were aware of their constituents' opposition to the Canal Treaties, but, since they did not regard those treaties as vital to the national security, they were vulnerable to White House pressure on the Panama vote. These Senators are likely to adopt a tougher position on SALT because they want to win back irate constituents and because they are worried that the Soviets grow stronger while the President weakens U.S. defense. Since it would not seem to be in the interests of either Carter or Brezhnev to sign an unratifiable arms treaty (unless Brezhnev wished to place the full blame for arms control failure on the United States), perhaps both sides were obfuscating and stalling so that SALT would not have to be debated in the Senate until after the November 1978 elections.[10]

The situation was further complicated in late August when it was reported that President Carter had instructed the U.S. SALT delegation in Geneva that he wanted the option of submitting SALT II to the Congress as an executive agreement (requiring a majority vote of both Houses) rather than as a treaty (requiring the assent of two-thirds of the Senate), and that the language of the draft text should be altered accordingly. Apparently the President had been advised by Secretary Vance and Arms Control and Disarmament Agency (ACDA) Director Paul C. Warnke, and warned by Senate Democratic leaders, that it would be unwise to offend the Senate by trying to by-pass it in this manner.[11] Nevertheless, as 1978 drew to a close the White House seemed insistent on retaining its options. It did not seem prudent for the President to irritate the Senate and perhaps alienate some of his own supporters by suggesting such an alternative possibility. If the Senators opposed to SALT II were to filibuster against an executive agreement, it would require 60 votes in a full chamber to close debate—only seven fewer than the number required for treaty ratification. It may have been the President's intention merely to trade the threat of pursuing a different route for a few crucial Senate votes. ("If you will assure me of your support, I will submit the agreement as a treaty.")

During 1978, the Carter Administration took steps to improve relationships with the domestic critics of SALT. It upgraded the role of Lt. General Edward Rowny, the representative of the Joint Chiefs of Staff on the SALT Delegation. It instituted a more effective system of reporting on SALT negotiations to the Congress, and welcomed the formation of a Senatorial advisory group to the SALT Delegation.[12] So confident was the Administration that a SALT agreement was within reach during the weeks of Carter's highest popularity and prestige after the Camp David meeting with Middle East leaders Anwar Sadat and Menachem Begin that officials were predicting that a Carter-Brezhnev Summit would occur in early December. Furthermore, it was announced that ACDA Director Warnke, a controversial figure who had been confirmed as chief U.S. arms control negotiator a year and a half earlier by the unimpressive Senate vote of 58-40, would resign from his post in a move widely interpreted as designed to enhance the prospects of ratification by allowing Secretary of State Vance, Secretary of Defense Harold Brown, and other officials to serve as Administration spokesmen in promoting the treaty.[13]

The view that President Carter was going to some lengths in order to ensure ratification was strengthened by his appointment of retired Lt. General George M. Seignious to succeed Warnke as head of ACDA (but not as SALT negotiator, a position assumed by Warnke's deputy negotiator, Ralph Earle). The appointment of Seignious, too, sparked a minor controversy when it became known that he had previously been associated with the American Security Council's Coalition for Peace Through Strength, an organization which had criticized the proposed SALT II Treaty on the grounds that it would make it impossible for the United States "to recover from a decade of unilateral disarmament."[14] After the November Congressional elections resulted in a net loss of three pro-SALT votes and an increase in the number of undecided Senators, it was not clear at year's end that the President could win a ratification fight, especially if the Egyptian-Israeli peace effort remained inconclusive and the Senate remained concerned over developments in Iran, the presence of Soviet MIG-23s in Cuba (in possible violation of the Kennedy-Khrushchev understanding of October 1962)[15], and the continuing Soviet military buildup.

FROM SALT I TO SALT II

It will be recalled that the SALT I Accords of May 1972 consisted of an Anti-Ballistic Missile (ABM) Treaty and an Interim Agreement covering strategic delivery vehicles. The ABM Treaty limited each side to the deployment of no more than 100 anti-ballistic missiles located at each of two sites—the national capital and one Intercontinental Ballistic Missile (ICBM) site.[16] The ABM Treaty is of unlimited duration, but under Article XV each side reserves the option of withdrawing, with six months' notice, if it decides that developments in the ABM area jeopardize its supreme interests. In 1972 the Soviets had ABM (the "Galosh" system) deployed around one site—Moscow—with some ICBMs bracketed within the protected area. The United States was beginning to deploy ABM around two ICBM sites—Malmstrom and Grand Forks. After the Treaty was signed, construction at Malmstrom was immediately discontinued. In 1974 Nixon and Brezhnev reached a further agreement discontinuing the additional one-site option, which each side had refrained from exercising.[17] Subsequently the United States got out of the ABM business entirely when Congress decided not to renew appropriations for the system at Grand Forks. The ABM Treaty is, of course, still in effect, but at the present time the United States is not doing anything about its one ICBM-site option. During the last year, the failure of the superpowers to negotiate a replacement for the Interim Agreement on Offensive Weapons (which expired on October 2, 1977), combined with growing concern about a continuing multi-dimensioned Soviet military buildup, has led to a revival of interest in both ballistic missile defense and civil defense programs as possible U.S. responses.[18]

The SALT I Interim Agreement covering strategic delivery vehicles set the following target figures for each side, to be reached after anticipated and permitted shifts from land-based to sea-based missiles had been made:

U.S.:   1,000 ICBMs, and 710 SLBMs on
            44 modern submarines
U.S.S.R.:   1,408 ICBMs, and 950 SLBMs on
            62 modern submarines

The Agreement thus recognized for the Soviets a 40% edge in the number of ICBMs and a 34% edge in the number of Submarine-Launched Ballistic Missiles (SLBMs). The Nixon Administration assumed that the United States could accept an agreement codifying its numerical inferiority at that time because: 1) the Agreement excluded strategic bombers, a category in which the U.S. then enjoyed an advantage (496 to 140); 2) the U.S. was thought to have deployed 5,700 strategic nuclear warheads while the Soviets had deployed 2,500; 3) the United States had access to three overseas bases at Holy Loch, Rota, and Guam, whereas the U.S.S.R. had none, thus making it easier for the U.S. to keep nuclear submarines on firing station;[19] and 4) the U.S. was presumed by nearly all strategic analysts to be qualitatively ahead of the Soviets in Multiple Independently Targeted Re-entry Vehicle (MIRV) technology, nuclear submarine and SLBM technology, and missile accuracy. Furthermore, the Agreement excluded 7,000 U.S. tactical nuclear warheads assigned to the NATO theater, along with the so-called forward based systems (e. g., the A-6As and the A-7s on aircraft carriers in the Mediterranean and the F-111s in Britain, which have a tactical role in NATO but which could conceivably strike targets on Soviet territory—aside from the issue of their ability to return to Western bases). The Soviets had sought to include these systems in SALT, but they refused to consider the inclusion of medium and intermediate range missiles stationed in Western Russia and targeted on Western Europe. Thus all European theater nuclear weapons (including British and French SLBMs) were left outside the scope of SALT I. (The Soviets did, however, attach to the SALT I Interim Agreement a unilateral statement reserving the right, if Britain and France should increase the number of their modern ballistic missile submarines, to carry out a corresponding increase.)

The most important part of the Interim Agreement from the American standpoint was a provision limiting the Soviets to 313 of the "heavy missiles" (SS-18 type) which Moscow was then in the process of deploying. (The term "heavy missile" was nowhere clearly defined, and this left room for much argument in subsequent years.) Despite this limitation, the Soviets under SALT I were assigned a sizable margin—variously estimated at four-to-one or six-to-one or greater—in total strategic "throw weight." It was feared by U.S. strategic analysts that such a basic quantitative superiority could become crucially significant in the future as the Soviets developed MIRV technology and made other qualitative improvements (e. g., in missile accuracy).[20] When the U.S. Senate approved the SALT I Interim Agreement in September 1972, it therefore attached the Jackson Amendment urging and requesting the President "to seek a future treaty that, inter alia, would not limit the United States to levels of intercontinental strategic forces inferior to the limits provided for the Soviet Union."[21]

Negotiations for SALT II began in Geneva in November 1972. At the Moscow summit meeting of June-July 1974, it was decided that it would be more realistic to work for an agreement which would last until 1985 in place of the permanent agreement originally envisaged. The United States engaged in a quest for a "conceptual breakthrough" in SALT throughout dismal days of foreign and domestic crisis which included a withdrawal from Southeast Asia in the wake of Watergate and the resignation of President Nixon. It proved extremely difficult to determine what would constitute "essential equivalence" in the strategic capabilities of the two superpowers, in view of their differing weapons systems, geostrategic requirements, and doctrines concerning the best way to deter the adversary.

The formula for "strategic parity" (if one is to be found) must take into account such factors as the number, location pattern, and range of launchers and missiles; the number of warheads; the elusive element of vulnerability and invulnerability (which is a function of hardening in the case of land-based ICBM silos, of alert status in the case of bombers, and of mobility and the state of Antisubmarine Warfare [ASW] and anti-ASW arts in the case of submarines); strategic intelligence concerning the location of targets; geodetic science; ballistic accuracy; terminal guidance; missile reliability; warhead yield; penetrability against available defenses; survivability of command, control, and communications; and other factors affecting the final kill capability. Of even greater importance and uncertainty are strategic doctrine; the actual plan of strategic operations intended by each side (which, of course, can never be a subject of negotiations); and a political-psychological assessment of what governmental leaders and their advisors may feel compelled to do, or constrained from doing, at various stages of a developing crisis or actual nuclear exchange. (More will be said below about asymmetries of strategic doctrine which make it extremely difficult to reach a SALT II agreement.)

THE VLADIVOSTOK AGREEMENT

In November 1974, the Ford-Brezhnev Agreement at Vladivostok established SALT II guidelines under which each side would be able to keep an agreed aggregate number (2,400) of strategic delivery vehicles of all types (including strategic bombers) and an agreed aggregate number of ICBMs and SLBMs equipped with MIRVs (1,320). Each side would presumably be free to determine its own mix among bombers, ICBMs, and SLBMs.[22]

One important difference between the SALT I Interim Agreement and the Vladivostok Agreement was that the latter included strategic bombers. The fact that the United States enjoyed a numerical advantage in bombers is probably what made an agreed launcher ceiling feasible.[23] The inclusion of strategic bombers made the Vladivostok numbers seem equitable, even though they did not involve any substantial alteration of the U.S.-Soviet ratio for strategic missiles agreed upon in SALT I.

Whereas SALT I had specified "fixed" land-based ICBMs, the language of the Vladivostok Agreement left the way open for mobile ICBMs, something which the United States had earlier opposed. Later there arose considerable confusion over whether the Vladivostok Agreement covered two emerging weapons technologies—the U.S. Cruise missile and the Soviet Backfire bomber. Apparently neither of these two systems had been discussed at Vladivostok, or taken into account in wording the agreement. The United States contended quite plausibly that the term "missiles" in SALT negotiations had always referred to *ballistic* missiles and therefore excluded Cruise missiles, which are air-breathing and not ballistic. (The Soviets for several years have had Cruise missiles known as "Shaddocks" deployed on submarines. To this day, the United States is not known to have made an issue of these weapons in the SALT negotiations, even though these missiles could possibly strike targets in U.S. territory more than 300 miles inland from any coast.) The Soviets naturally wanted to include Cruise missiles and exclude Backfire bombers. They contended that Backfire was a tactical bomber, having a range of only 1,300 miles; U.S. estimates of its capability were considerably in excess of that, however, and indicated that the bomber has the ability to hit U.S. targets and land in Cuba.[24] Because of the impasse over Cruise and Backfire, the Ford Administration was unable to make further substantial progress in the SALT negotiations.

THE CARTER PROPOSAL OF MARCH 1977

When the Carter Administration assumed office, it decided that the most serious problem to be addressed in SALT was the growing vulnerability—in view of the deployment of Soviet heavy missiles potentially equipped with MIRVs—of the U.S. land-based ICBM force. While the Soviets at the time of SALT I had not yet acquired a MIRV capability, within a few years they had tested at least four new land-based missiles, three of them with MIRVs, and two MIRVed SLBMs. Washington was particularly concerned that large numbers of SS-18s, each with eight to ten warheads and large payloads, could develop the theoretical potential in the 1980s of knocking out the land-based leg of the U.S. deterrent in one blow. The Carter Administration, reflecting a new concern over technological developments which had begun to materialize during the Nixon-Ford years, therefore decided to adopt a different tack in the arms talks.[25]

In March 1977, the United States made a two-option proposal to the Soviets. Option I was a comprehensive package calling for major cuts (up to 25%) in the Vladivostok ceilings. It would: 1) limit aggregate numbers of strategic weapons of all types to between 1,800 and 2,000; 2) reduce the number of heavy missiles permitted the Soviets from more than 300[26] to 150; 3) lower the MIRVed launcher limit from 1,320 to 1,100 or 1,200, of which no more than 550 could be land-based ICBMs (the same number already MIRVed by the United States); 4) control the rate of qualitative weapons improvement by limiting ICBM and SLBM tests to a total of six per year, and halt entirely the deployment of follow-on systems; 5) ban the deployment of all Cruise missiles with a range in excess of 2,500 kilometers, and limit Cruise missiles deployed on non-heavy bombers, submarines, and ships to a range of 600 kilometers; 6) count the Backfire bomber as a tactical rather than a strategic system; and 7) ban all mobile land-based missiles (MX).[27] In sum, the United States was willing to accept limits on Cruise and set aside its objection to Backfire in return for a major reduction (more than 50%) in the projected number of Soviet heavy missiles. The Administration estimated that Option I, if accepted, would cut the Soviet throw-weight advantage from 3:1 to 2:1, and this latter ratio was deemed tolerable and compensable. Option II was a fairly tough posture which said in effect to the Soviets: if you insist on ignoring our concern over the threat which your heavy missiles pose to our ICBMs, then we will go back to the Vladivostok guidelines, but we will exclude both Cruise and Backfire from the negotiations, and defer those systems to a later round.

The Soviet Union, not surprisingly, flatly rejected the American two-option proposal. The super-secretive Kremlin was obviously irked, first of all, by President Carter's decision to go public with the general thrust of the U.S. plan before the Moscow talks had commenced. If the Soviets thought that it might be a mere ploy to give the new Administration time to become acquainted with the inward intricacies of SALT, they gave no indication of such thinking. Moscow roundly scored

Option I as marking a substantial departure from guidelines earlier agreed upon by Brezhnev and Ford, and called it a blatant effort by the United States to gain a "unilateral advantage." (Logically, one could brand an effort to reduce the Soviet advantage from 3:1 to 2:1 an attempt to achieve a "unilateral advantage," but the Soviets could hardly regard such an effort as unprecedented in the history of diplomatic negotiations.) The Soviets found Option II unacceptable probably because they assumed that the United States was less genuinely concerned over the Backfire bomber than they themselves were over the future potential of Cruise missiles.[28]

In an effort to keep the arms talks alive and to move toward an agreement before the SALT I expiration deadline in early October 1977, the United States modified its proposal. The new plan called for: 1) a cut of only 150 in the ceiling of 2,400; 2) a freeze, starting in October, on the further emplacement of MIRVs in Soviet SS-18s (estimated to be about 200 by that time); 3) an agreement by the Soviets not to exceed a total production of 250 Backfires by 1980 (a number which the U.S.S.R. probably cannot exceed in any event, at least not at the rates of production of about 30 per year which have obtained since 1974); 4) a retention of the earlier U.S. proposals on limits for the Cruise; 5) a ban on the deployment (but not the development and production) of mobile missiles such as MX and SS-16; and 6) an agreement to refrain from testing new generation ICBMs and to limit each side to six ICBM shots per year.[29]

No breakthrough occurred, however, in the negotiations before the SALT I Interim Agreement expired on October 3, 1977. The two governments agreed that they would continue to abide by the agreement until the completion of a SALT II Treaty—on the basis of reciprocity, of course. Negotiations continued through 1977 and 1978, against the background of a deteriorat-

ing detente (discussed at the outset of this paper). The
Carter Administration was meanwhile accused by
Moscow of preparing to step up the "arms race,"[30] in
spite of the U.S. decisions to cancel the B-1 bomber and
to put the development of the neutron bomb (enhanced
radiation weapon) on "hold." Concern continued to
mount in the United States over the Soviet strategic and
European theater military buildups, and questions were
raised in Congress about Soviet compliance with the
SALT I Accords and about U.S. ability to verify
compliance with SALT II, if an agreement were to be
signed.[31] Several analysts were moved to express
disillusionment with the whole concept of arms control
negotiations, describing them as exercises which may
have served a useful purpose in the past but which may
now have the effect of exacerbating rather than alleviat-
ing tension, of speeding up rather than slowing down
the pace of armaments competition.[32]

CURRENT SALT NEGOTIATIONS

The actual text of the SALT II Agreements was still
confidential as this paper went to press. When Secretary
Vance met Foreign Minister Gromyko in July and
September, he carried with him a proposed text running
to more than fifty pages. Some of the details—probably
the most important ones—of the clauses already agreed
upon have been made public either through government
reports or background briefings to Congressmen, journalists, and others. Judging from a variety of sources,[33]
the tentative SALT II Agreements seem to have the following shape:
1) There is to be a Treaty covering aggregate ceilings and
   sub-ceilings which will be in effect until 1985; an
   interim Protocol for two to three years covering
   issues not ready for long-term resolution; and a
   Statement of Principles to govern SALT III.

2) The main provisions of the Treaty are as follows:
   a) The initial aggregate level of 2,400 launchers is to be reduced to 2,250 during the term of the Treaty or Protocol. This means a cut of 250 in the existing Soviet arsenal, none in the U.S. arsenal.
   b) There will be a sub-ceiling of 1,320 for all MIRVed ICBMs, SLBMs, and heavy bombers equipped with long-range Air-Launched Cruise Missiles (ALCMs); a sub-ceiling of 1,200 on total numbers of land-based and sea-based MIRVed missiles; a sub-ceiling of 820 on the number of MIRVed ICBMs; and a sub-ceiling of 313 on Soviet heavy SS-19s.
   c) Any missile of a type tested with MIRV will be counted as a MIRVed vehicle when deployed.
   d) The testing and deployment of long-range ALCMs are to be restricted to heavy bombers (B-52s, Bear, and Bison).
   e) ALCMs deployed on heavy bombers may be limited to a range of 2,500 kilometers (defined to include an additional 30 percent in order to permit a zig-zag course). In October 1978 it was reported that the Soviet Union had offered to eliminate the range restriction on U.S. ALCMS, provided that the United States would agree to extend temporarily the range limits on Ground- and Sea-Launched Cruise Missiles, as defined in 3d) below, by moving that provision from the shorter-term Protocol into the Treaty, thereby keeping these restrictions in effect until 1985. This poses a serious problem for U.S. alliance diplomacy (see "The NATO Allies and SALT" below). In January 1979 it was not known what the final outcome would be.
   f) To prohibit rapid reloading of ICBM silos (with "popup" or "cold-launch" missiles that do not destroy the silo on lift-off), the storage of excess missiles at launching sites is to be prohibited.
   g) Each side agrees not to circumvent the agreement by transferring technology to other parties (allies).

h) Both sides shall provide prior notification of missile testing and information on size and performance of arsenals, and both shall refrain from interfering with national means of verification.

3) The proposed Protocol would:

a) Ban the testing and deployment of new types of missiles, with certain exceptions (which are still being argued over);

b) Ban qualitative improvements in existing systems, provided such a ban could be verified;

c) Place some restrictions on the testing and deployment of new mobile ICBMs, but not on the testing from fixed launchers of ICBMs which might later be mobile; and

d) Ban the flight testing and deployment of any Cruise missiles of more than 2,500 kilometers range (measured by ground distance, allowing for a zig-zag course), and ban the deployment of Cruise missiles of more than 600 kilometers range on sea-based or ground-based launchers. (Thus only Air-Launched Cruise Missiles of 2,500 kilometers range could be deployed during the life of the Protocol.) If the Soviet proposal described in 2e) above should be accepted, the United States would not be permitted to deploy longer-range Ground-Launched Cruise Missiles (GLCMs) and Sea-Launched Cruise Missiles (SLCMs) until 1985.

As 1978 drew toward a close, the following issues appeared to be the outstanding ones awaiting settlement in SALT:

a) The length of time the Protocol would remain in effect (with the United States favoring expiration in December 1980 and the Soviets holding out for three full years after SALT II goes into effect). The United States also wanted the U.S.S.R. to cut back to the allowed total of 2,250 strategic missiles by the end of 1980, whereas the Soviets sought to delay that deadline until mid-1982.

b) Methods of verifying compliance with SALT II provisions (against a background of rising Congressional concern on this score). In November 1978, the U.S. Government said that the U.S.S.R. by encoding the telemetry of SS-18 tests—i. e., concealing or disguising the electronic signals on flight performance transmitted from the missile's guidance unit to ground stations—would make it more difficult for the United States to monitor compliance with the provisions of SALT II banning qualitative improvements in weapons. (In 1972, the two parties had agreed not to interfere with each other's ability to verify compliance through national detection means. Since SALT I contained only quantitative limitations, the United States was generally satisfied with intelligence gathered by reconnaissance satellites. SALT II, however, will place limits on missile modernization, such as increasing the number and perhaps accuracy of warheads on a single missile. This will require additional, sophisticated means of gathering information on Soviet testing programs, and will probably lead to disagreements over the interpretation of what constitutes interference with each other's verification process.)

c) The allowable methods of deploying Air-Launched Cruise Missiles (with the Soviets insisting that ALCMs could be launched only from heavy bombers, each of which must be limited to twenty missiles and counted as a MIRVed launcher, while the United States wants the option of using wide-bodied cargo planes capable of carrying up to sixty or more ALCMs, as well as fighter-bombers). At one point the United States proposed an average number of thirty-five Cruise missiles on ALCM-carrying planes, but the Soviets continued to insist upon a maximum of twenty on each carrier. There was another issue involving Cruise missiles on which the two superpowers were at loggerheads. The United States held that only ALCMs with nuclear warheads would be limited. The U.S.S.R. wanted to count planes carrying any Cruise missiles, whether conventionally or nuclearly armed, because of the difficulty of verifying the difference and also because a conventional Cruise missile is a U.S. "strategic" weapon if it can strike Soviet territory.

d) The precise manner in which the Backfire bomber will be treated (whether in the Protocol, or in a letter from Brezhnev to Carter, and what kind of guarantee, of whatever worth, will be involved—e.g., an assurance that the Backfire will be deployed at bases out of range of the United States and that Backfire crews will not be trained in in-flight refueling). It has been reported that one of the ways in which the United States might deal with the Backfire bomber would be to announce that it reserves the right during the lifetime of the SALT II accord to develop and deploy a new bomber with similar characteristics.

e) The types of new missile systems which can be tested and deployed, including mobile missiles. The latter issue seems to have become the principal stumbling block in the negotiations, and deserves separate treatment in this paper.

MOBILE MISSILES

As indicated previously, many American strategic analysts and Senators have become worried in recent years about the growing vulnerability of the U.S. land-based ICBM force to a Soviet first strike. Early in the Summer of 1978, the Carter Administration appeared to accept the Defense Department argument that

SALT II must leave the United States free to reduce the threat to the land-based leg of the deterrent triad. It was taken for granted that without such freedom a finished treaty could not be ratified by the Senate. (Whereas the Soviets have deployed hundreds of new missiles during the last five years, the "youngest" Minuteman silo is now more than ten years old. Moreover, the B-1 bomber was cancelled in favor of the Cruise missile, but the average age of the B-52s—the system on which Air-Launched Cruise Missiles will depend—is well over twenty years, and those bombers will be poised against air defenses that are not constrained by SALT.)

Several suggestions were made for dealing with the problem of ICBM vulnerability: e. g., phase out land-based missiles and put them at sea; put ICBMs on heavy-lift helicopters; put 200 to 300 MX missiles on tracks in ten- to fifteen-mile long tunnels protected underground; or move the 200 to 300 new ICBMs around 4,000 to 6,000 empty silos in random fashion, thereby creating in effect a "shell game" which would make it impossible for Moscow to target American land-based missiles in a first-strike strategy.

For about a year the Pentagon had apparently favored the underground tunnel approach, but that was finally abandoned on the grounds that it would be too costly, that it would be difficult to find uninhabited areas (amounting to the size of Connecticut) in which tunnels of such length could be constructed, and that even if such a system could be built it might still prove vulnerable to attack. The "shell game" thus emerged as the preferred approach early in the Summer of 1978. The very fact that Secretary Vance carried such a novel plan to Geneva in July 1978, when the negotiations were allegedly so close to the final stage, was evidence of poor planning in the fields of national defense and arms control. The Soviets, probably anticipating a U.S. proposal for MX, had earlier offered to give up the testing and deployment of one new single warhead missile through 1985 if the United States would forego the MX, but the latter had become much more important for Washington than the former was for Moscow. The Carter Administration seemed to have two different options in mind: 1) to build additional silos for hiding existing Minutemen; and 2) to keep the door open for the development of a larger, more advanced MX.[34] The Soviets, of course, objected strongly to the U.S. proposal for the deployment of mobile ICBMs, citing the difficulty of verifying that the large number of silos housed only a small number of missiles.[35]

Critics of MX contended that even though Minutemen might be vulnerable to a 90 percent wipe-out by the mid-1980s, the United States would not need MX and the Soviets could not carry out a first strike because they would still have to worry about retaliation from submarine- and bomber-launched weapons. These critics also feared that the Soviets would also demand the right to build a comparable number of decoy silos, and would target the U.S. ICBM force with the largest warheads possible. It was even suggested that, if necessary, the U.S. could adopt the policy of "launch on warning," a policy which most advocates of arms control in the past have regarded as dangerously destabilizing. Nevertheless, Air Force General David C. Jones, Chairman of the Joint Chiefs of Staff, declared that the United States needs the mobile missile or MAP (for multiple aimpoint) deployment to counter the threat of increasingly accurate Soviet re-entry vehicles.[36] Defense Secretary Harold Brown later suggested that the United States would not sign a SALT II accord that prevented the development of an alternate launch point system for Minuteman.[37] Generally speaking, advocates of a deterrent triad saw little merit in the argument that the owner of the triad did not have to worry if one of the three legs folded up.

Subsequently, yet another U.S. plan to reduce ICBM vulnerability came to the fore, when a White House

Scientific Panel chaired by Dr. Frank Press recommended the adoption of a plan to deploy hundreds of missiles on airplanes which would be able, in event of attack, to land at any of some 2,000 dispersed airstrips throughout the country. Under this "land and launch" alternative, nuclear missiles would be placed on tractor-trailer trucks carried inside large C-5 transports (and later in quicker takeoff aircraft), normally stationed at Strategic Air Command bases. If a crisis arose, the planes would be deployed to smaller air bases where the truck could move to pre-surveyed locations from which trained crews would prepare the missiles for launching within an hour. Advocates of the plan argued that it would give rise to fewer political and environmental problems than the MAP program, but they admitted that it suffered from deficiencies: vulnerability of the planes to attack; inaccuracy of targeting due to haste of firing; difficulties of command and control in the chaos of an actual attack (when several hundred commercial aircraft would be trying to land at their nearest airfield); and the temptation it would pose to the U.S.S.R. to develop more lethal thermonuclear weapons for a preemptive strike.[38] It can also be plausibly argued that for invulnerability this plan requires an even longer warning time than would the present ICBM force under a "launch on warning" policy, and that opponents of its $40-50 billion cost might press for the adoption of such a policy as a surer and cheaper alternative. The Administration was thus deeply divided on the best way to reduce ICBM vulnerability—and this seemed to constitute a major weakness in U.S. strategic planning during what were hailed as crucial penultimate phases of the SALT II negotiations. The confusion was not dispelled by the Administration's request for funding the MX in the supplemental military budget request.[39]

THE NATO ALLIES AND SALT

The European allies of the United States, heavily dependent for their security upon the American nuclear deterrent, have always been sensitive to adverse shifts in both the global strategic balance and the European theater balance. As U.S. superiority gave way to "parity," the European balance became more important than it had been before, when it was assumed that U.S. tactical nuclear weapons in NATO could adequately compensate for Warsaw Pact conventional strength. For several years now, the West Europeans have been worried about the adversary's substantial superiority in armor (19,000 to 20,000 tanks compared to NATO's 6,000 to 7,000). When Mutual and Balanced Force Reduction (MBFR) talks began in Vienna five years ago, NATO's prime objective was to cut the Soviet edge in armor. Three years ago, NATO offered to trade some of its tactical nuclear weapons for an entire Soviet tank army. In November 1977, NATO weakened its demands: the East could withdraw its tanks and tank crews from any Warsaw Pact units on the Central European front. The Soviets in the meantime were accumulating European theater nuclear capabilities at a rate that alarmed the West Europeans. Throughout the era of "strategic parity" the Europeans heard increasingly frequent references to the possibility of "decoupling" European defense from the U.S. nuclear deterrent, and worried about the future "Finlandization" of Western Europe. In June 1978, the Soviets suggested that they might be interested in the Western plan to trade 1,000 NATO nuclear weapons for 1,700 Warsaw Pact tanks.[40] Many Europeans were not enthusiastic about a plan that might in effect place a ceiling on NATO nuclear arms and no comparable ceiling on Soviet nuclear arms at a time when the latter were being deployed in the European theater in increasing numbers. At times the Europeans have worried that the two

superpowers might conclude SALT agreements detri-
mental to the interests of Western Europe. They would
be probably more disturbed, however, by a collapse of
the SALT negotiations than by the conclusion of an
agreement which would receive broad Senate approval
after a debate in which the interests of the NATO allies
had been fully considered. The Europeans have been
pleased that the United States has managed to keep the
so-called forward-based systems of NATO outside the
scope of SALT, despite repeated Soviet efforts to
include them. In recent years the Europeans have been
particularly concerned about two Soviet weapon
systems—the Backfire bomber and the SS-20. Even if
the United States finally decides not to regard Backfire
as a strategic threat, the Europeans certainly do. SALT
II, moreover, will do nothing to alleviate European
apprehensions concerning the SS-20 missile; this missile
remains outside the definition of a "strategic weapon"
since, without being strapped to its third rocket stage, it
does not threaten the United States. It can, however,
easily reach targets in Western Europe.[41] European
voices are now being heard calling for a new arms
negotiating forum capable of dealing with all nuclear
weapons systems—the so-called gray area systems
deployed in the European theater—which are not being
treated either in SALT or MBFR.[42]

West European defense specialists have been afraid
that the United States might try to obtain concessions
on strategic missiles from the Soviets by bargaining
away Cruise missiles.[43] The Europeans regard Cruise as
of great potential significance for their future security,
for it is viewed as a means of rectifying the theater
imbalance. They thus want to retain the option of
acquiring long-range, highly accurate Cruise missiles for
launching from air, ground, and sea. While the Europeans are technically capable of developing Cruise on
their own, they do not wish to diverge from U.S.
objectives in SALT, since this might increase the

probability of a "decoupling" of European defense and American deterrence. Acquisition of Cruise in cooperation with the United States and within a NATO context is therefore viewed as preferable.

The Europeans hope that the United States will be extremely careful in wording the non-circumvention or no-transfer provisions of SALT II, and that it will not accept permanent limits on the range of Cruise which would reduce the defense problem for the Soviets by confining the threat to a clearly demarcated area. Realizing that it will take a few years to develop Cruise to an operational stage, they can accept (if they must) a U.S. pledge not to transfer Cruise technology during the life of a two-or-three-year Protocol. Their principal objection to such a Protocol clause is that the Soviets will strive to establish the presumption that the temporary curb is a permanent one, and that the United States will be unwilling to alter course when the Protocol expires, since this will be portrayed as a reversal of SALT II and will enable the Soviets to deploy new strategic missile systems now being developed. To allay European fears, the United States is now considering the development of a new long-range European theater missile for NATO.[44] While Administration sources were exuding optimism in December 1978 that a Carter-Brezhnev summit was again moving into view as a result of strides being made in the SALT negotiations, Secretary Vance in London sought to reassure the NATO allies that a strategic arms agreement would enhance rather than weaken Western security.[45]

SALT, STRATEGIC DOCTRINE, AND THE SENATE

SALT is not the only arms forum. In Vienna, Geneva, and elsewhere, the superpowers are negotiating about MBFR, a comprehensive test ban, restraints on developing antisatellite destroyers, a chemical weapons ban, naval arms limitations in the Indian Ocean, and limits on the transfer of conventional arms. It is not possible to review here the progress, or lack thereof, in these other arms control negotiations. SALT is, without question, the most important arms control arena, and its outcome will affect the developments in other areas.

Scarcely anyone now doubts that, regardless of how much the United States and the Soviet Union may be committed to deterrence and arms control, their approaches to these twin concepts are quite different as a result of their differing strategic doctrines. Whereas U.S. doctrine, developed by civilian strategists, calls for each side to place restraints upon its ability to destroy the strategic retaliatory capabilities of the other, Soviet strategic doctrine, developed by military leaders, does not presuppose such restraint but requires instead a maximum ability to blunt the nuclear striking power of the adversary if war should break out—and, indeed, to strike preemptively if nuclear war should seem imminent.[46]

It is not clear whether two superpowers which have long subscribed to such divergent strategic doctrines of deterrence and arms control can arrive at an agreement equitable in its consequences even if not symmetrical in its provisions. Theoretically, such an outcome is possible—but only if the two sides fully understand the defense implications of the differences between them, and not if one side officially and naively insists that both parties are bound to approach SALT from the same set of philosophical and strategic premises.

A SALT II agreement which restricts one side substantially more than the other, and prevents it from taking steps which are deemed essential to its security and to a continuing international strategic equilibrium, will in the end serve only to exacerbate suspicion, fear, and tension, and will be in danger of collapsing before SALT III can be negotiated. If an agreement is initialed, it is important that it be of the sort with which both sides can live comfortably until 1985. Up to now, the Soviet Union has sought to pursue its own interests through a process of very tough bargaining; and for this, no one can fault the Soviet negotiators. Governments are responsible for the security of their people; they need not apologize for driving the hardest bargain they can get. The American people have a right to expect a manifestation that their own government has acted with a similar sense of responsibility and concern. The American people do not want to hear a lot of rhetoric about SALT II as a "centerpiece of detente" (under which rubric it has hitherto been oversold) or as a great saver of money in the defense budget (which it is not likely to be). The American public does want to be convinced that SALT II will genuinely strengthen mutual deterrence, that it will fairly enhance the security of both superpowers and place neither at a military disadvantage, and that it will in the long run contribute to a more stable and peaceful world. All persons who are interested in intelligent and prudent arms control within this kind of framework will be looking for an agreement that can command overwhelming confidence and support on the part of Congress and the public alike, not an accord that will squeak by narrowly after an acrimonious debate that leaves the country deeply divided.

The American people cannot possibly master all the technical details of SALT II. Confused by the acronyms and the numbers, they will properly look to the Senate for an unhurried, penetrating, and reasoned debate—one in which the inevitable shibboleths, dissembling, naive illusions, and simplifications hopefully will be minimized. Whatever agreement is reached ought to be scrutinized most carefully, certainly in each specific clause but even more so in its comprehensive significance for the Unites States, its allies, and the future good of mankind. One caveat is in order. If we happen to disagree with the underlying assumptions of U.S.

strategic doctrine during the last quarter century and with the weapons choices flowing from that doctrine, we should not assess the blame upon SALT II, so long as SALT does not prevent us, within the framework of strategic parity, from correcting those past deficiencies and mistakes which now give us cause for serious worry.

NOTES

1 *The New York Times*, July 31, 1978.
2 *Ibid.*, June 1, 1978.
3 *Ibid.*, June 18, 1978.
4 Bernard Gwertzman, "U.S. Reported Acting to Strengthen Ties with Peking Regime," *ibid.*, June 24, 1978. The Soviet Politburo said that China is a serious threat to peace, is involved in expansionist action, works for an uncontrollable arms race, and seeks access to NATO military arsenals. Dusko Doder, "Soviets Warn West Against Arms Sales to Peking," *Washington Post*, August 27, 1978.
5 Drew Middleton, "Military Gains for China Seen in U.S. Ties," *New York Times*, December 18, 1978; David K. Shipler, "Threat to Detente Seen in China Links," *ibid.*; Martin Tolchin, "Carter Says Soviet Accepts China Step," *ibid.*, December 20, 1978; David K. Shipler, "Soviet Wary About U.S. Pledge China Tie Has No Hostile Intent," *ibid.*; Richard Burt, "Chinese Card: How to Play It," *ibid.*; David K. Shipler, "Soviet, Citing Its Note to Carter, Indicates Concern on China Ties," *ibid.*, December 22, 1978; Kevin Klose, "Soviets Dispute Carter Version of Brezhnev Note," *Washington Post*, December 22, 1978; David K. Shipler, "Soviet Denies Foot-Dragging on Arms Pact," *New York Times*, December 27, 1978; Terence Smith, "Carter and European Leaders Seek to Assure Soviet on Ties to China," *ibid.*, January 7, 1979; "An Interview With Brezhnev," *Time*, January 22, 1979; and David K. Shipler, "China Has People, U.S. Has Machines, Russia Has Fear," *New York Times*, January 28, 1979.
6 "Now Carter is in the Dock with Shcharansky," *Manchester Guardian Weekly*, July 16, 1978. Some Senators called for a suspension of the SALT negotiations because of the trials. Henry L. Trewhitt, "SALT Deal Opposed by Senators," *Baltimore Sun*, July 12, 1978.
7 See the editorial, "Tough Talk Is No Substitute for a Fair Arms Agreement," *Louisville Courier Journal*, April 2, 1978.
8 *The New York Times*, February 12, 1978.
9 Senator Robert C. Byrd of Virginia, Democratic majority

leader, said: "It's better not to have agreement than to have a bad one, to bring a treaty here and have it rejected." Senator Alan Cranston of California, assistant Democratic leader, said that a two-thirds vote for an arms treaty would be "impossible this year" and "very, very tough" next year. Adam Clymer, "Senators Cautious on an Arms Accord," *ibid.*, April 20, 1978.

10 See Godfrey Sperling, Jr., "Senate Set to Turn Down SALT Pact," *Christian Science Monitor*, April 17, 1978; Henry L. Trewhitt, "The Senate Looms Large Now as an Obstacle to SALT," *Baltimore Sun*, June 11, 1978; and William Beecher, "U.S. Holding Steady on SALT," *Boston Globe*, June 2, 1978.

11 See Henry L. Trewhitt, "Executive Accord Weighed for SALT," *Baltimore Sun*, August 26, 1978; Bernard Gwertzman, "Carter's Hill Strategists Weigh End Run to Get SALT Pact Approval," *Washington Star*, August 25, 1978; and Robert G. Kaiser, "Byrd Warns Administration SALT Pact Must Be a Treaty," *Washington Post*, August 26, 1978.

12 Stephen J. Flanagan, "Congress, the White House and SALT," *Bulletin of the Atomic Scientists*, Vol. 34 (November 1978), pp. 34-40; Kevin Klose, "Senators, Soviets Debate Arms Limits," *Washington Post*, November 16, 1978.

13 Robert G. Kaiser and Don Oberdorfer, "U.S. and Soviets Reported on Verge of SALT II Pact," *Washington Post*, October 6, 1978; Kenneth H. Bacon, "Warnke Quits Arms Control Post in Move Seen Prelude to Conclusion of SALT Pact," *Wall Street Journal*, October 11, 1978.

14 Bernard Weinraub, "Arms Unit Nominee Held Controversial," *New York Times*, November 10, 1978.

15 Henry L. Trewhitt, "U.S. Links Soviet Bombers in Cuba to 1962 Accord," *Baltimore Sun*, November 16, 1978; Charles W. Corddry, "U.S. Photo Planes Check Cuban MIG's," *ibid.*, November 17, 1978; "MIG-23's in Cuba," Editorial, *Washington Star*, November 21, 1978.

16 For the text of the ABM Treaty, see *Arms Control and Disarmament Agreements* (Washington: U.S. Arms Control and Disarmament Agency, June 1977), pp. 132-135.

17 For the text of the ABM Protocol, see *ibid.*, pp. 149-150.

18 See *The Emerging Strategic Environment: Implications for Ballistic Missile Defense*, A Conference Report (Cambridge, Mass.: Institute for Foreign Policy Analysis, 1978). In November 1978, President Carter called for more than doubling civil defense spending over the next five years, at a total cost of $2 billion in that period. He proposed a program based not on the construction of fallout shelters but rather on the preparation for rapid evacuation of cities in time of crisis. Richard Burt, "Carter Adopts a Program to Bolster Civil Defense in Nuclear Attack," *New York Times*, November 13, 1978.

19 This is undoubtedly one reason why President Nixon and

Secretary Kissinger expressed concern about the possibility than the Soviets might obtain a base in Cienfuegos, Cuba. That would have upset the SALT I naval balance. Later, U.S. strategists would also be concerned over reports that the Soviets were deploying at sea SLBMs of longer range—longer not only than U.S. Poseidon missiles, but even than the projected Trident.

20 There was mounting concern among U.S. analysts that even if the Soviets would not dare use their quantitative margin to plan a deliberate first strike, they might nevertheless project throughout the world an image of military superiority which would have very adverse political consequences for the West.

21 *Documents on Disarmament 1972* (Washington: U.S. Arms Control and Disarmament Agency, 1974), p. 653.

22 The official text of the Joint United States-Soviet Statement of November 24, 1974 mentioned only "agreed aggregate numbers" without specifying what they were, in obvious deference to the Soviets' penchant for secrecy. The numbers were made public a short time later in a press conference by President Ford.

23 Richard Burt, "SALT After Vladivostok," *The World Today*, February 1975, p. 59.

24 The CIA assigns to the Backfire a range of 3,500 miles and calls it "tactical." McDonnell-Douglass analysts, using information supplied by the Defense Intelligence Agency, concluded that with in-flight refueling Backfire could achieve a range of 4,500 to 6,000 miles. See John M. Collins, *American and Soviet Military Trends Since the Cuban Missile Crisis* (Washington: Center for Strategic and International Studies, Georgetown University, 1978), Notes 6 and 7 on p. 19. Collins, however, says that while Backfire may have a bearing on U.S. needs for improved air defense, it does not raise U.S. offensive requirements. *Ibid.*, p. 109.

25 Hedrick Smith, "Carter Said to Accept Implicitly Pentagon View on Heavy Missiles," *New York Times*, April 5, 1977; George C. Wilson, "U.S. Goal in Arms Plan: Reducing Threat of a First Strike," *Washington Post*, April 5, 1977.

26 The number permitted in SALT I was usually reported as 313. In recent years, reports have referred to slightly different figures. The discrepancy may be due to problems of counting, and to the fact that the Soviets insist that launchers and missiles used for test firing should not be counted.

27 Before Secretary Vance took the proposal to Moscow, President Carter in a press conference announced that the United States would seek "deep cuts." This chagrined the Soviets, who later revealed some of the numerical details of the U.S. plan. See *The New York Times, The Washington Post*, and *The Baltimore Sun* for April 6, 7, and 8, 1977; and *Time*, April 4 and 11, 1977.

28 *Strategic Survey 1978* (London: International Institute for

Strategic Studies, 1978), p. 94.

29 William Beecher, "U.S. Proposes 6-Point Plan to Save Arms Talks," *Boston Globe*, June 12, 1977.

30 For a reasoned argument that the United States has not been engaged in a genuine arms race with the Soviet Union since the early 1960s, see Albert Wohlstetter, "Is There a Strategic Arms Race?", *Foreign Policy*, No. 15 (Summer 1974) and "Rivals, But No Race," *ibid.*, No. 16 (Fall 1974).

31 Since SALT I, the United States has officially raised questions concerning Soviet compliance and possible violations in the following areas: 1) the construction of ICBM silos beyond the number permitted; 2) deliberate concealment of strategic weapons; 3) testing an air defense system radar in an ABM mode; 4) failing to dismantle old ICBMs as new SLBMs were deployed at sea. The Soviets also raised questions about shelters over Minuteman silos, deactivated Atlas and Titan-I launchers, radar on Shemya Island, and dismantling of ABM radar at Malmstrom Air Force Base. On February 21, 1978 Secretary Vance assured the Senate Foreign Relations Committee that all these questions have been satisfactorily resolved between the two parties. Vance noted other press accusations, never officially discussed, relating to the blinding of U.S. satellites, Soviet deployment of mobile ABMs and ICBMs, Soviet encoding of missile test telemetry, and the development of anti-satellite destroyers. Two days later, Paul C. Warnke, Director of the Arms Control and Disarmament Agency, forwarded to the same Committee a report stating that the anticipated SALT II agreement is adequately verifiable by existing national technical means; that undetected cheating might be possible, but not enough to alter the strategic balance; and that it could be discovered in time to make an appropriate response. *Department of State, Selected Documents No. 7.*

32 See, for example, Edward N. Luttwak, "Why Arms Control Has Failed," *Commentary*, Vol. 65 (January 1978), pp. 19-27; and Richard Burt, "Arms Control and Soviet Strategic Forces: The Risks of Asking SALT to Do Too Much," *The Washington Review of Strategic and International Studies*, Vol. 1 (January 1978), pp. 19-31. See also Richard Burt, "Treaties That Slow the Arms Race Usually Speed It Up," *New York Times*, December 24, 1978.

33 See especially *Arms Control 1977* (Washington: U.S. Arms Control and Disarmament Agency, May 1978), p. 9; *The Strategic Arms Limitation Talks*, Department of State Special Report No. 46, July, 1978; *World Armaments and Disarmament*—SIPRI Yearbook, Stockholm International Peace Research Institute (London: Taylor and Francis, 1978), pp. 430-436; Richard Burt, "The Scope and Limits of SALT," *Foreign Affairs*, Vol. 56 (July 1978), especially pp. 756-760; Bernard Gwertzman, "Warnke Has New U.S. SALT Ideas,"

Washington Star, September 7, 1978; David Linebaugh, "When Vance Meets Gromyko on SALT," *Christian Science Monitor*, September 13, 1978; Kenneth H. Bacon, "Issues Blocking SALT Pact Are Unlikely To Be Resolved During Talks in Moscow," *Wall Street Journal*, October 20, 1978; Richard Burt, "Hopes for Early Arms Accord Fade in Washington," *New York Times*, November 7, 1978; and Vernon A. Guidry, Jr., "For Some SALT II Experts, Encrypting Is A Vital Issue," *Washington Star*, December 15, 1978.

34 See Bernard Weinraub, "Defense Chief Backs Start on a System of Mobile Missiles," *New York Times*, October 6, 1977, and "U.S. Predicts Threat to its Missile Force," *ibid.*, November 6, 1977; Richard Burt, "U.S. Aides Push for Random Deploying of Missiles," *ibid.*, June 18, 1978, and "U.S. to Insist on Mobile Missiles in a Soviet Pact," *ibid.*, July 9, 1978; and William Beecher, "Vance Will Tell Russians Missile-Site Option a Must," *Boston Globe*, July 12, 1978, and "Abroad: a Proposal on SALT," *ibid.*, July 13, 1978.

35 "Soviet Objects to U.S. Missile Plan, Complicating Talks on Arms Pact," *New York Times*, July 24, 1978.

36 George C. Wilson, "Joint Chiefs Chairman Says U.S. Needs a Mobile Missile," *Washington Post*, July 26, 1978.

37 Don Oberdorfer, "U.S. to Retain 'Shell Game' Missile Option, Brown Says," *ibid.*, August 23, 1978. ACDA Director Paul C. Warnke, in response to arguments that the MAP would be inconsistent with verification provisions, said that SALT agreements limit "launchers," not launch points or silos. Don Oberdorfer, "Missile 'Shell Game' Is Consistent with SALT, Warnke Says," *ibid.*, August 25, 1978; Bruce Ingersoll, "The Old Shell Game: Can U.S. Play it in Deploying Missiles?", *Chicago Sun-Times*, November 12, 1978.

38 Bernard Weinraub, "Plan for Airborne Missiles to Land Before Firing Arouses U.S. Debate," *New York Times*, November 21, 1978; George C. Wilson and Walter Pincus, "Diverse Deployments Seen Protecting Big Land Missiles," *Washington Post*, November 21, 1978.

39 Richard Burt, "Pentagon Includes Two New Missiles in Its 1979 Budget," *New York Times*, November 14, 1978; and "White House Speeds Action on Mobile Missile, Hoping to Aid Arms Pact," *ibid.*, December 21, 1978.

40 Richard Burt, "Soviet Offers Plan for Reducing Forces in Central Europe," *New York Times*, June 13, 1978.

41 Richard Burt, "The SS-20 and the Eurostrategic Balance," *The World Today*, February 1977.

42 See Lothar Ruehl, "The 'Grey Area' Problem," in *The Future of Arms Control: Part I—Beyond SALT II*, edited by Christoph Bertram, Adelphi Paper No. 141 (London: International Institute for Strategic Studies, Spring 1978), and "NATO

Europeans Call for a Say in the Drafting of SALT III," *Atlantic Community Quarterly*, Vol. 16 (Spring 1978).

43 Bernard Weinraub, "NATO Voices Concern Over Plans to Limit Cruise Missile Range," *New York Times*, October 13, 1978.

44 Walter Pincus, "Hill Conferees Authorize Development of Long-Range Ballistic Missile System," *Washington Post*, August 3, 1978; Takashi Oka, "New Missile to Counter Soviets for NATO?", *Christian Science Monitor*, August 29, 1978.

45 Bernard Gwertzman, "Vance Assures NATO Soviet Arms Accord will Help Security," *New York Times*, December 10, 1978; Richard Burt, "Strides in Arms Talks Said to Bring Summit Session Near," *ibid.*, December 11, 1978; and Bernard Gwertzman, "U.S. and Soviet Appear Near a Tentative Agreement on Limits for Strategic Arms," *ibid.*, December 23, 1978

46 Stanley Sienkiewicz, "SALT and Soviet Nuclear Doctrine," *International Security*, Vol. 2 (Spring 1978); John Erickson, "The Chimera of Nuclear Deterrence," *Strategic Review*, VI (Spring 1978); Fritz W. Ermarth, "Contrasts in American and Soviet Strategic Thought," *International Security*, Vol. 3 (Fall 1978).

2

The Merits and Demerits of a SALT II Agreement

Paul H. Nitze

The following essay is drawn from an address given by Mr. Nitze before a Defense Strategy Forum sponsored by the National Strategy Information Center in Washington, D.C. on November 15, 1978.

Six years ago, in the Fall of 1972, the United States entered into the second round of Strategic Arms Limitation Talks (SALT) with the Soviet Union. What the U.S. hoped to achieve in these negotiations was a treaty of indefinite duration limiting offensive nuclear strategic armaments. This treaty, it was hoped, would parallel the Anti-Ballistic Missile (ABM) Treaty which had recently been negotiated and ratified and which had just entered into force. The positive objectives the U.S. sought in such a treaty were three:

a) Limitations consistent with the actuality and appearance of rough parity (i.e., equivalence) in the offensive strategic nuclear capabilities of the two sides; and

b) Limitations such as would assure maintenance of stability in a crisis threatening the outbreak of war—i.e., force deployments such that neither side could expect to gain, relative to the other superpower, by striking first.

c) It was the further hope of the U.S. that both sides—having assured these objectives—could then proceed to reduce the resources devoted to nuclear armaments, and that the weight of nuclear armaments on world politics would therefore be lessened.

The United States recognized that in pursuing these objectives a number of constraining factors would also have to be taken into account:

a) The agreed provisions strategically important to the U.S. should be reasonably verifiable by the available means of inspection;

b) The interests of U.S. allies should be considered and the terms of the agreements should be acceptable to them;

c) The force levels permitted should be low enough so that it would be economically and politically feasible for the U.S. to deploy those forces permitted by the agreements and necessary to achieve the objectives of parity and stability; and

d) The agreements must be negotiable, for if they are not acceptable to the Soviet Union and ratifiable by the U.S. Congress, there can be no treaty.

From the beginning, the United States realized that questions must be raised and addressed with respect to the priorities, emphases, and trade-offs among these constraints and positive objectives. It was recognized that no single consideration was absolute, and that the various factors must be analyzed together. The U.S. hoped, however, to do at least as well as it had with the ABM Treaty, which, while not perfect, was considered to be equitable in its terms and useful in its over-all results. *Over the years, however, it has become increasingly clear that one aspect of the fourth constraint—i.e., that the agreements be acceptable to the Soviet side and thus be negotiable—has come to dominate all other considerations.*

The SALT II agreements—as now all but finally

agreed upon—fall short of the original U.S. objectives in many ways, including the following:

The first casualty was the goal of achieving a treaty of unlimited duration to parallel the ABM Treaty. This objective was jettisoned at the Moscow meeting in the Summer of 1974, where the U.S. and the U.S.S.R. agreed to pursue the more narrow objective of a ten-year agreement which would expire in 1985. It still has not been decided whether the main agreement is to be a treaty or an executive agreement, although there is much reason to believe that the Senate will insist that the treaty procedure be followed.

The second casualty was parity, or essential equivalence. As the SALT II negotiations now seem to stand, the appearance—but not the actuality—of equal limitations is preserved. Both sides, for example, are permitted 820 MIRVed ICBMs, but within that limit the Soviets can have over 300 very large modern missiles while the U.S. is permitted none. More importantly, there is no possibility that the U.S. will or can deploy more than 550 MIRVed ICBMs, as opposed to the permitted 820, prior to the expiration of the treaty. As another example, the Soviets are permitted four, six, and ten warheads respectively on their SS-17, -19, and -18 missiles, while the U.S. is permitted only three on its Minutemen III. The United States is permitted up to ten warheads on a new ICBM, but it is virtually certain that such a missile will not be deployed by 1985. It is agreed that the Soviet Backfire will not be counted under the over-all ceiling, and that similar American planes will also not be counted. The Soviets are expected to have some three or four hundred Backfires by 1985, however, while it is virtually certain that the U.S. will have no such planes beyond its present much smaller FB-111s.

Even more significant than the sacrifice of rough parity is the sacrifice of crisis stability. Up to the present time, the situation has been such that an

American attack on Soviet ICBM silos or a Soviet attack on American silos would be unprofitable, for it would require the use of a far larger portion of the attacker's ICBMs than the proportion of the defender's silos which would be eliminated by the strike. By the early 1980s, if present trends continue, this will no longer be true, for the Soviets could then expect to destroy some 90 percent of U.S. ICBM silos while using only a third or so of their MIRVed ICBMs. Most American bombers on-alert and submarines at-sea would survive, but the residuals left to both sides would hardly be equivalent in war fighting capabilities.

Under the present proposals, another American positive objective—reductions in the resources devoted to nuclear armaments—will also fail to be accomplished. Few, if any, serious observers assert that SALT II would result in a reduction of expenditures for strategic nuclear forces by either the U.S. or the U.S.S.R.

The aims of the first three constraints have also been substantially compromised:

While much effort has gone into attempting to make the provisions of SALT II appear to be verifiable, the task of verification will be almost impossible if the Soviet side tries purposefully to evade verification. Because of the difficulty in verifying missile production or storage, concentration has been placed largely on limiting the number of launchers. Those Soviet silos using the cold-launch technique, however, are reloadable in a day or two if they are not directly attacked in the interim period, while those using the hot-launch technique are reloadable in a few days longer. Missiles in storage can be erected and fired from soft pads, the number and location of which are virtually unverifiable.

While the United States has tried to take the interests of its allies into account, the likely agreements treat the so-called gray area systems—which are of great importance to U.S. allies—in a most inequitable way. The Soviet SS-20s—which are mobile, accurate, and most threatening to all positions within arcs some two to three thousand miles from the Soviet perimeter—are not limited. Cruise missiles with a range greater than 600 kilometers are, however, the subject of various limitations, and the transfer of such Cruise missiles and their technology to U.S. allies appears to be a matter of debate.

The aim of the third constraint—i.e., that the limitations be such that it is politically and economically feasible for the U.S. to deploy permitted systems up to the level necessary to preserve equivalence and crisis stability—has also been eroded. As noted earlier, the U.S. is permitted 820 MIRVed ICBMS, but there is virtually no possibility that the U.S. can deploy more than 550 by 1985.

The fourth constraint—that the agreements be negotiable—has, over the years, out-weighed all the U.S. positive objectives and the other three constraints. Making the provisions of the agreements acceptable to the Soviet Union has come to dominate all other considerations, but the other aspect of the requirement of negotiability—that the agreements be ratifiable by the Congress of the United States—also has had an impact on the negotiations. One result of this important factor has been a dramatic opposition in the information and propaganda objectives of the two sides.

From the time of the initial SALT I negotiations, the Soviet Union has mounted a vigorous, multifaceted propaganda effort to persuade the world, including Americans, that the U.S.S.R. is uniquely devoted to peace, has been the initiator of every imaginative move toward peace, and is the threatened party surrounded by potential enemies who are plotting the encirclement of the Soviet Union. This campaign has consistently depicted the United States as making excessive demands and refusing to make the necessary compromises for agreement.

The U.S. government has generally avoided responding to these charges, in part because it was confident that the charges were wholly untrue and contrary to fact and would therefore be unpersuasive to most objective people at home and abroad. Additionally, the U.S. government has been engaged in another type of propaganda campaign of its own: persuading the American people and the U.S. Congress that SALT II should be ratified. This campaign has led the Arms Control and Disarmament Agency, and many of ACDA's supporters in and out of government, to present positions characterized less by objectivity than by advocacy, wishful thinking, and emotion. The Soviet Union is faced with no similar problem with respect to Soviet public opinion, and can direct its public information campaign toward a single target—the United States.

Outside ACDA, the mainline of the Executive Branch's argument in favor of ratification of SALT now appears to stress three points. The first reflects a reduced claim as to what SALT II will accomplish. While it is no longer claimed that SALT II will assure rough parity in strategic offensive capabilities or assure crisis stability, proponents of the accord assert that it will be better than no agreement. The second point is an emphasis on the importance of keeping the SALT negotiating process functioning, for it is maintained that it should be possible in SALT III to achieve many of those things which it has not been possible to achieve in SALT II. Additionally, it is claimed that the U.S. side has not been idle, and that SALT II will be no bar to the prompt initiation and further development of those programs necessary, prudent, and practical to assure the adequacy of the American deterrent posture.

How accurate is the assertion that the SALT II agreements will better serve U.S. security interests than no agreement at this time? Proponents of the SALT II accords point out that the draft treaty calls for a limit, to be reached by January 1, 1982 or thereabouts, of 2,250 on the number of strategic launchers and heavy bombers on both sides. Since the Soviet Union presently has some 2,500 launchers, it will thus have to phase out approximately 250 to come down to this limit. Furthermore, the Soviet Union has a number of ICBM and SLBM programs underway, as well as a heavy bomber program. In the absence of an agreement, so this argument goes, the Soviets might well deploy some 400 additional new launchers and heavy bombers without phasing out any existing weapons. The U.S., on the other hand, currently has less than 2,250 launchers, has no systems in production or development that could raise the American total much over 2,250 by 1985, and will thus be required to make no reductions.

Secondly, advocates point out, the SALT II treaty will put a ceiling of sorts on the aggregate missile throw-weight Soviet launchers can launch and a ceiling of sorts on the aggregate number of missile re-entry vehicles the Soviets can deploy. These limits, it is claimed, will be particularly helpful to the U.S. if it proceeds with a multiple aimpoint system (MAPS) deployment, designed to assure the survivability of American ICBMs.

There are, however, counterarguments to both of these assertions. With respect to the first, it should be noted that the missiles which the Soviets will be required to phase out are becoming obsolete in any case, and their retention would add little to Soviet capabilities. It is also not clear what contribution 400 additional new missiles would make to the Soviet position. If such a contribution can be made, a cheaper way of accomplishing that objective would be for the Soviets to add 400 missiles to their stockpile and use them for silo reloads or for launch from soft pads.

The strategic importance of the second argument depends on whether or not the United States will in fact proceed with MAPS or a similar deceptive ICBM basing mode. From the point of view of this writer, the MAPS issue has become crucial to whether or not a SALT II accord, from the strictly military/technical point of view, will be better or worse than no agreement. The question of whether or not a MAPS deployment is consistent with the already agreed-upon provisions of SALT II is not clear. The deployment of mobile ICBMs is to be banned during the period of the Protocol, but it appears that deployment of a mobile system would be permitted after the expiration of the Protocol. It has been reported, however, that the Soviets have serious reservations with respect to an American insistance that a MAP system (which in some deployment schemes may not strictly be a mobile system) could, in fact, be deployed under the terms of the Treaty after the expiration of the Protocol. The Executive Branch has apparently decided not to press for further clarification, and instead appears to be studying alternatives which do not raise this question. Many observers believe these alternatives have already been studied to death and found to be unsatisfactory. Perhaps it will be the case that before it announces initialing of an accord, the Executive Branch will be able to throw more light on the crucial issue of how it proposes to go about assuring the survivability of the ICBM component of the American deterrent. If the Executive Branch does not clarify this area of concern, the issue will surely be a crucial part of the ratification debate.

What emphasis should be placed on the importance of keeping the SALT negotiating process functioning? Is it likely that it will be possible to accomplish in SALT III those objectives and aims which could not be achieved in SALT II? In approaching these questions, it is useful to review again what has occurred over the six years of SALT II negotiations. The U.S. has made little progress toward its initial objectives. The negotiations have eventually turned on agreement on minor adjustments to the programs each side had already determined to carry out. The Soviet side, for its part, had determined to replace its third generation ICBMs with fourth generation systems. In accomplishing this aim, the Soviets were determined to maintain their advantage in ICBM throw-weight and to equal or exceed the U.S. in the accuracy, MIRVing, and other aspects of ICBM technology. The Soviets were also determined to equal or exceed the U.S. in the number, range, and degree of MIRVing of SLBM systems, and to equal the U.S. in the technology of their defensive systems. The likely SALT II agreements do not appear to stand in the way of Soviet movement toward the achievement of any or all of these objectives.

On the other side, the United States had opted for a much more modest program, partially for budgetary reasons but also because there was much doubt as to the need or wisdom of adding to the sheer size of American strategic forces. The B-1 bomber program was cancelled independently of SALT. There has been slippage in the Trident and MX programs, also quite independently of SALT. The United States has proceeded during the period of the SALT negotiations with those programs to which it was committed: completion of the Poseidon conversion program, execution of the Minuteman III deployment and modernization program, and development of Air-Launched Cruise Missiles (ALCMs). With minor modifications, SALT II tends to legitimize and to some extent freeze those programs for the next six years.

The process of negotiations has thus turned out to be one of negotiating small changes in Soviet programs for small changes in U.S. programs. As one looks forward to the SALT III negotiations, what developments seem possible or likely which will change the very nature of the SALT process? It is difficult to imagine what those developments will be, unless the U.S. manages in the interval to change present trends in the evolving relationship of U.S. strategic forces to those of the Soviet Union. Again the United States is faced with the importance of correcting the growing vulnerability of the land-based component of its strategic missile forces. There have been stories in the press that the Executive Branch has proposed to ask for funds for two new missile programs; neither, however, would be ready for deployment before the expiration of SALT II.

SALT is at the intersection of three realms: the military/technical, the diplomatic/negotiating, and the psychological/propaganda/political. The interaction of these realms is extremely important. If the SALT II agreements are initialed before the crucial issues are thrashed out, before a consensus is developed with respect to these issues, and before a reasonable prospect for Congressional ratification is determined, the United States will incur serious risks in the psychological/propaganda/political field. The Soviet propaganda apparatus will certainly assert that the Executive Branch's approval of the SALT agreements attests to the accord's equity and contribution to peace. It will be difficult for the Executive Branch to deny these assertions, and to argue that the agreements are merely the best which could be accomplished under adverse negotiating circumstances. Failure of the Congress to ratify the SALT II treaty could thus result in a difficult political and propaganda problem for the United States worldwide. Furthermore, another consideration will enter the debate. The President of the United States will have committed his prestige to a crucial negotiation with the Soviet Union. The question will arise as to whether, in these difficult and dangerous days, Congress should not back the President, even though in many respects Congress might wish to withhold ratification.

For all these reasons, it is important that the issues be debated now, before SALT II is initialed. A continuation of the negotiations while the United States gets its house in order would be better than excessive haste in arriving at an agreement which may later be regretted.

The following sections consist of major portions of a paper by Mr. Nitze originally distributed by The Committee for the Present Danger.

A. THE SALT II NEGOTIATING POSTURE IN JANUARY 1979

The negotiations are intended to produce a SALT II Treaty, a Protocol, and a Statement of Principles.

THE SALT II TREATY

The Treaty is to run to December 31, 1985. The significant points regarding its contents are as follows:

a) The aggregate number of strategic nuclear launch vehicles (SNLVs)*—i.e., launchers for ICBMS, launchers for SLBMs, "heavy bombers," plus air-to-surface ballistic missiles (ASBMs) with a range greater than 600 kilometers—is to be limited initially to 2,400 each for the U.S. and the Soviet Union. By some particular date, now reported to be in 1982, the initially authorized limit of 2,400 SNLVs is to be reduced to 2,250.

b) Within the permitted aggregate number of SNLVs, a sublimit of 1,320 will be placed on the number of launchers for ICBMs carrying MIRVs, plus launchers for MIRVed SLBMs, plus aircraft equipped to carry armed Air-Launched Cruise Missiles (ALCMs) with a range greater than 600 kilometers (which are also to be counted under the SNLV ceiling as "heavy bombers").

c) A sublimit of 1,200 is to be placed on the number of MIRVed ICBM launchers plus MIRVed SLBM

---

*The phrase strategic nuclear delivery vehicles (SNDVs) is often, but less precisely, used to describe this aggregate.

launchers.

d) A sublimit of 820 is to be placed on the number of MIRVed ICBM launchers. Within this 820 limit, the Soviet Union will be allowed a number of fixed modern large ballistic missile (MLBM) launchers equal to the present Soviet force level, which is 308 (or 326 if 18 operational MLBM launchers at the Soviet test range are counted). The United States, which has no fixed MLBM launchers, will be permitted none in the future. New ballistic missiles with useful payloads (throw-weight) greater than that of the Soviet SS-19 will be considered to be MLBMs, and ballistic missiles with useful payloads greater than that of the Soviet SS-18 will be banned.

e) The rules governing what missile boosters are to be considered boosters for MIRVed missiles and governing what launchers are to be counted as launchers for MIRVed missiles have been established. Any missile booster of a type which has been tested with MIRVs is to be considered a MIRVed missile booster. Any launcher of a type from which a MIRVed missile booster has been launched will be considered a launcher for MIRVed missiles. Agreement has not been reached on what is meant by "type."

f) Limited modifications of existing types of ICBMs are permitted. Any test of an ICBM with more re-entry vehicles (RVs) than has been previously tested on that type of missile will, however, cause it to be classified as a "new type." The U.S. has tested seven RVs on the Minuteman III on two occasions, although it is deployed with only three RVs. It has recently been reported that the Soviet Union has accepted the U.S. position with respect to preserving the option for deployment of seven RVs on Minuteman III without such a variant counting as a "new type." There are, however, no plans to proceed with the deployment of such a variant. In any case, the deployment of seven substantially lower yield RVs on Minuteman III would not increase the aggregate hard target kill capability of Minuteman IIIs so equipped over Minuteman IIIs each equipped with three Mark-12A warheads. The Soviet Union has tested four RVs on the SS-17, six RVs on the SS-19, and ten RVs on the SS-18. Testing of certain other types of modifications will also cause an ICBM to be classed as a "new type." The sides have agreed that each side will be permitted to flight test and deploy one "new type" ICBM (MIRVed or un-MIRVed) during the Treaty period. There is no limit to the number of "new type" SLBMs which the sides are permitted to test and deploy during the life of the Treaty. It has recently been reported that the Soviet side has requested a further exemption from the "new type" rule for missiles smaller than the missiles they would replace.

g) The Soviet side is reported to have agreed that during the period of the Treaty there be a ban on the flight testing and deployment of a larger number of RVs on any "new type" ICBM missile than the largest number already flight tested by either side on any of its ICBMs (i.e., 10) and on its SLBMs (i.e., 14). The Soviets have agreed with the U.S. position that the maximum fractionization of RVs for SLBMs be limited to fourteen RVs per missile. There is now agreement by both sides that the number of ALCMs carried on a single aircraft is to be similarly limited, although the specific number of ALCMs per aircraft (approximately 30) has not yet been agreed.

h) As a general rule, the U.S. B-52s and B-1s and the Soviet Bears and Bisons are to be counted as "heavy bombers" and will thus be counted under the ceiling on SNLVs. Any bomber or transport aircraft equipped to carry armed ALCMs with a range greater than 600 kilometers is also to be counted as a "heavy bomber." If an aircraft is equipped to carry more than the agreed maximum number of ALCMs per aircraft, it will be counted as being an appropriate multiple of one "heavy bomber" under the 1,320 limit.

i) Both sides are now agreed that the Soviet Backfire bomber is not to be counted as a "heavy bomber" (unless it were to be equipped to carry ALCMs of range greater than 600 kilometers).

1) The Soviet Union is reported to have agreed to make an informal declaration, outside the contractual forms of the Treaty, of its intention not to raise the production rate of the Backfire above the current rate of about thirty per year, and not to use it in an intercontinental strategic role. The U.S., for its part, will declare its intent to retain the option of producing and deploying a new penetrating bomber of a type similar to Backfire which would also not be counted against the SNLV limit.

2) With respect to Soviet "heavy bomber" variants—these include Bears and Bisons reconfigured to reconnaissance, tanker, and antisubmarine roles—the U.S. position has been that only a portion of them, to include Bisons reconfigured as tankers, should be counted as SNLVs. The Soviet position has been that none should be so counted. It is reported that the U.S. has now agreed to the Soviet position.

3) It has been the position of the United States that any aircraft may be equipped to carry ALCMs with a range greater than 600 kilometers, but such aircraft must then be counted, not only against the SNLV limit, but also against the 1,320 limit. It has been the Soviet position that, other than heavy bombers (currently in-

cluding Bears, Bisons, B-52s, and B-1s), only transport aircraft newly constructed for the specific purpose of carrying ALCMs may be equipped to carry ALCMs. It is now reported that the Soviet position has been accepted.

j) Cruise missile range is defined as the maximum distance the missile can achieve, measured by projecting its flight path onto the earth's surface. The operational range, after allowing for zigs and zags to avoid defenses, will thus be significantly less than the defined range. With respect to ICBMs, intercontinental range is specified as being 5,500 kilometers or more. No specification has been agreed as to the range cutoff distinguishing SLBMs classed as SNLVs and submarine-launched missiles considered to be for tactical use only.

k) The Soviet position is that during the period of the Treaty, the deployment of armed (including both conventionally and nuclear armed) Ground- and Sea-Launched Cruise Missiles (GLCMs and SLCMs) with a range greater than 600 kilometers will be prohibited. The U.S. position is that this ban should apply only during the duration of the Protocol.

l) There are no limits on the number of missiles or warheads which may be produced and stored. ICBMs in excess of those needed for permitted launchers, and storage facilities for such ICBMs near launching sites, are, however, to be prohibited. The development, testing, and deployment of rapid reload systems for ICBM launchers are also to be prohibited.

m) Both sides are agreed that there will be a commitment that neither side will take any action which would circumvent the purposes of the agreements. Such a provision would appear to ban the significant transfer to third nations of weapons limited by the agreements. The extent to which this provision would ban the transfer of components or technology is not clear. The Soviet interpretation has been reported to include the transfer of components, blueprints, and technology directly pertinent to such weapons in such a ban.

n) Agreement has been reached on obligations for reciprocal disclosures of pertinent data. The Soviet Union has made certain data available and has agreed that additional information will be made available.

o) Agreement has been reached on obligations to refrain from interfering with techniques unilaterally controlled by the respective sides for verification of one another's performance. Both sides have agreed not to encrypt information they judge necessary to the other for adequate verification of matters limited by the agreement.

p) The start of additional and the relocation of existing fixed ICBM launchers are to be banned.

THE PROTOCOL

The United States has proposed that the terminal date of the Protocol be June 30, 1981. It is reported that the Soviet Union has proposed that the terminal date be in 1982.

The only significant restriction in the Protocol, beyond those restrictions in the Treaty, concerns mobile ICBMs, ASBMs, and launchers for armed Ground- and Sea-Launched Cruise Missiles:

a) The flight testing or deployment of mobile ICBMs and of ASBMs is to be banned during the period of the Protocol. After the expiration of the Protocol, the Treaty language, unless then amended, would permit the development, testing, and deployment of mobile ICBMs and of ASBMs, but launchers for each such missile would have to be counted under the pertinent limits. Both sides apparently are agreed that the testing of mobile launchers for mobile ICBMs during the Protocol period is not prohibited, provided that no missile is fired from such launchers. It has been reported that the Soviets have raised serious concern over an American insistence that a multiple aimpoint (MAP)* system (which is more precisely a transportable, rather than a mobile, system) would be permitted under the terms of the Treaty after the expiration of the Protocol.

b) During the period of the Protocol the deployment of armed GLCMs and SLCMs with a range greater than 600 kilometers will be prohibited. (If this provision is included in the Treaty it will not be required in the Protocol.)

THE STATEMENT OF PRINCIPLES

The Principles are to serve as guidelines for the negotiations for the next stage in SALT. These negotiations are anticipated to follow-on soon after the completion of SALT II.

a) The United States has proposed the following principles, or targets:

1) A reduction in the aggregate number of SNLVs.
2) A reduction in the MIRVed missile launcher limit.
3) Provisions further restricting the development, testing, and deployment of new ICBMs and SLBMs.
4) Provisions restricting the flight testing of ICBMs and SLBMs.

---

*The U.S. Air Force now prefers the name "Multiple Protective Structure" (MPS) system; see General Lew Allen's letter of December 29, 1978 to the Chairman of the House Armed Services Committee.

5) Further restrictions on strategic defenses, including air and civil defenses.
6) Steps to strengthen verification through "cooperative measures," in addition to "national technical means."

b) It is the position of the Soviet Union that such a Statement of Principles should make clear that the U.S. and allied theater nuclear weapons capable of reaching the U.S.S.R. must be taken into account in arriving at new ceilings; that the subject of restrictions on strategic defenses beyond those contained in the ABM Treaty is not appropriate for SALT; and that no "cooperative measures" other than those in support of "national technical means" should be considered.

B. CONSIDERATIONS BEARING ON THE MERITS OF SALT II

The following analysis deals with the principal considerations involved in arriving at a judgment on the merits of the agreements as they appeared to be emerging from the negotiating process at the end of 1978, and in view of the different strategic nuclear programs of the two sides.

THE ICBM BALANCE TO BE EXPECTED BY 1985

The MIRVed ICBM Balance

This component of the overall balance is of particular significance. It is likely that if deterrence fails, this component, because of its power and accuracy, its short time of flight, the greater reliability of its command and control, and its known location, would be the key element in an initial strike and any initial counterforce response. This exchange could well determine the military outcome of the war.

1) The United States has closed down the Minuteman III production line and has delayed the initial operating capability (IOC) date of a follow-on missile to 1986 or beyond. Therefore, there is essentially no possibility that the U.S. will have any deployed MIRVed ICBM launchers by the expiration date of the Treaty in 1985 other than the 550 Minuteman III silos currently deployed. The accuracy of the Minuteman III has recently been significantly upgraded, and the U.S. plans to substitute Mark-12A warheads (with approximately double the yield) for the Mark-12 warheads currently deployed on the Minuteman III. No other significant changes in Minuteman III are now planned. The useful payload of the Minuteman III is approximately 2,200 pounds, and the maximum number of re-entry vehicles (RVs) it can carry is three. The aggregate useful payload (throw-weight) of the U.S. MIRVed ICBM force in 1985 will therefore not exceed 550 times 2,200 pounds, which equals approximately a million and a quarter pounds. The aggregate number of MIRVed ICBM warheads in the U.S. force will not exceed 550 times three RVs, which equals 1,650 RVs.

2) The U.S.S.R. is permitted by the proposed terms of the agreements to deploy in excess of 300 SS-18s and approximately 500 SS-19s and -17s. The SS-18s have a useful payload approximating sixteen thousand pounds, and the SS-17s and -19s have a useful payload approximating seven to eight thousand pounds respectively. The SS-18s have been flight tested with as many as ten RVs, the SS-17s with four RVs, and the SS-19s with six RVs. It can therefore be anticipated that the aggregate throw-weight of the Soviet Union's MIRVed ICBM force will approximate eight to nine million pounds by 1985, and that the number of RVs deployed on these MIRVed missiles will approximate six thousand, each RV having a yield several times that of the U.S. RVs. There is no reason to believe that the accuracy of the Soviet

MIRVed RVs by 1985 will be significantly less than that of the improved accuracy of the Minuteman III RVs. The U.S. is developing its more radical accuracy improvement, the Advanced Inertial Reference System (AIRS), for incorporation in a new follow-on missile to be deployed after 1985.

3) If current Soviet accuracy is no better than approximately a fifth of a mile, it would be difficult for the Soviets to eliminate more than 70 percent of U.S. Minuteman silos in an initial strike, assuming that each silo is targeted with two RVs. If Soviet accuracy approximates fifteen hundredths of a mile, around 90 percent of U.S. silos would be vulnerable to such a two-on-one attack. A two-on-one attack would require less than half of the MIRVed ICBM RVs the U.S.S.R. is expected to have available by 1985. When Soviet accuracy approximates a tenth of a mile, around 90 percent of American silos will become vulnerable to an attack by a single RV against each silo, provided that additional RVs are programmed to substitute for missiles that fail during their launch phase.

4) If the United States were to use all its Minutemen III, it is unlikely—even taking into account improved accuracy and the substitution of Mark-12A for Mark-12 RVs—that the U.S. could destroy more than 65 percent of the Soviet ICBM silos.

The UnMIRVed ICBM Balance

The utility of large, single RV, unMIRVed ICBMs—which can have very high megatonnage and thus very high fallout potential—is largely as terror weapons to deter the other side from using its surviving deterrent in a second strike.

1) Until 1985 or beyond, the U.S. is expected to have 450 Minutemen II, each with a throw-weight of less than two thousand pounds and each carrying a single RV in the megaton range. These would give the U.S. approximately a million pounds of throw-weight and

550 megatons of yield in its unMIRVed Minuteman ICBM force. In addition, Washington may choose to maintain the fifty-four Titan missiles which were deployed prior to 1965. These missiles have an aggregate yield of some 450 megatons.

2) In coming down to the 2,250 limit, the Soviet side can be expected to retain at least 360 non-MIRVed ICBMs during the life of the Treaty. Since it is now reportedly agreed that each side will be allowed to test and deploy one new type of ICBM (MIRVed or non-MIRVed) during the period of the Treaty, it is likely that the Soviet side, having little need for a new MIRVed ICBM, will test and then deploy a new non-MIRVed ICBM with a throw-weight of approximately eight thousand pounds and a warhead yield of fifteen to twenty megatons, and substitute it for approximately 360 of the currently deployed SS-11s. The aggregate throw-weight of such an unMIRVed ICBM force could be in excess of two and one-half million pounds, and its megatonnage could reach approximately six thousand megatons.

THE SLBM BALANCE BY 1985

SLBM forces at-sea are particularly difficult to find and destroy and can be expected to endure beyond the initial exchanges. They should, therefore, be prime candidates for being held back as strategic reserve forces to influence the later phases of a war or to influence the period of war termination and beyond. It is not expected that SLBMs will achieve high accuracy by 1985. Additionally, the reliability of SLBM communications constitutes a continuing problem.

MIRVed SLBMs
The U.S. is scheduled to have the following MIRVed SLBMs by 1985:

a) Twenty-one Poseidon boats will each have sixteen missiles, each missile carrying eight to ten RVs, with the yield of each RV being forty kilotons.
b) Ten Poseidon boats will each be "backfitted" with sixteen Trident I missiles, each missile carrying approximately eight RVs. Each missile will have a substantially longer range (4,000 miles), and each RV will have more than double the yield of the forty kiloton Poseidon RV.
c) Seven Trident boats will each carry twenty-four Trident I missiles.

It was thus expected that the U.S. would by 1985 have 38 nuclear-propelled MIRVed SLBM submarines with some 664 MIRVed tubes with a theoretical loading of 5,312 RVs. Some 60 percent of these might be at-sea at any given time, giving the U.S. 3,200 RVs at-sea. Assuming a reliability rate of 80 percent, this amounts to approximately 2,550 at-sea reliable RVs, representing an aggregate yield of approximately 200 megatons. In the event of a crisis, it should be possible, in a number of days, to increase the at-sea force by some 25 percent.

The Soviet side—if Moscow deploys close to the full 820 MIRVed ICBM launchers permitted under the MIRVed ICBM limit—will be able to deploy nearly 400 MIRVed SLBM launchers and still stay within the 1,200 limit on MIRVed missile launchers. It is expected that the new Soviet Typhoon submarine will be significantly larger than the present Soviet SLBM submarines and will carry twenty to twenty-four missiles, each with up to fourteen RVs; the smaller Soviet MIRVed SLBMs, the SS-N-18s, are expected to have no more than half that number of MIRVs. The Typhoon missile could have the throw-weight of the projected U.S. Trident II missile, development of which has not yet been authorized. The Trident II missile is planned to be approximately twice the size (volume) of the Trident I missile, but will not be deployed prior to 1985.

It is probable, nevertheless, that the U.S. will continue to have a lead in the number of MIRVed SLBM tubes and RVs into the 1985 time period. However, the accuracy and yield of the American SLBM RVs are substantially less than those on the U.S. ICBMs. The U.S. SLBM force does not now, and is not by 1985 expected to, add significantly to American capability against Soviet hard targets, such as hardened silos.

UnMIRVed SLBMs

The U.S. is expected to phase out at least half of its unMIRVed Polaris force by about 1985 and thus to have no more than 80 unMIRVed SLBMs by that time.

The Soviet Union, on the other hand, can be expected to retain over 600 unMIRVed SLBM tubes. Some of these may carry multiple, but not independently guided, RVs (MRVs), as U.S. Polaris missiles do today. Such missiles may be useful as MIRVed missiles against small area targets that are not very hard, such as airfields.

THE BOMBER/CRUISE MISSILE BALANCE BY 1985

The essential characteristic of the bomber/Cruise missile forces is that while, particularly on the U.S. side, they have great potential power, it is only that portion of the force that is on alert prior to the initial attack that can be expected to survive, and unless the bulk of even that portion of the force is used within the initial eight hours of a nuclear war, it too runs the danger of being lost.

The B-1 issue was incorrectly presented by the Carter Administration as centering around a choice between relatively cheap Cruise missiles and expensive B-1s. Cruise missiles must be launched from some kind of survivable platform, preferably one that can endure in a nuclear war environment for more than a few hours. The position of the Executive Branch is that preferably this should be an aircraft. Thus, what is required is a bomber/Cruise missile system consisting of bombers and tankers so based as to give a high probability of pre-launch survivability for those that are on alert, whose takeoff is sufficiently rapid, and which are so hardened against nuclear effects that it becomes difficult to barrage their escape routes; bombers that are able to penetrate close enough to the target to launch Cruise missiles to destroy or suppress defenses; and Cruise missiles able to penetrate area and terminal defenses and accurate enough to kill the targets they are aimed at. Cruise missiles are thus only part of a multifaceted system, for the bombers that launch the missiles and the tankers that refuel the bombers are equally essential components. The system is greatly improved and the enemy's defensive problem is greatly increased if some of the bombers have the capability for rapid takeoff, are hardened against radiation, are more confidently able to penetrate Soviet defenses, and are thus able to launch Short-Range Attack Missiles (SRAMs), other types of missiles, or gravity bombs close to the target.

Since the B-1 program has been cancelled, the 1985 bomber/Cruise missile balance depends critically upon whether a Soviet barrier defense against U.S. B-52s is possible around the northern perimeter and on the eastern and western flanks of the Soviet Union; upon the number of Cruise missiles that will be able to penetrate new Soviet terminal defenses; upon the number of B-52s equipped with Cruise missiles that the U.S. deploys; upon the prelaunch and escape survivability of U.S. B-52s and their tankers; and upon the extent to which a portion of the bomber force can be reconstituted, after it is flushed on warning, so as to endure in a war environment protracted for more than a few hours.

Without limitations on air defense systems, including forwardly deployed, area, and terminal defenses, the effectiveness of U.S. Cruise missiles may be degraded during the mid- to late 1980s. Limitations on air defenses are not to be included as a part of the SALT II agreements and there is a question as to the willingness of the Soviets even to discuss this issue as part of the SALT III negotiations.

The U.S. contemplates deploying some 120 aircraft equipped with intermediate range ALCMs. It is planned that the majority of these aircraft will be B-52s; however, some type of transport aircraft carrying a larger number of ALCMs than does a B-52 is also being considered. If an aircraft is equipped to carry more than an agreed maximum number of ALCMs per aircraft, it will be counted as being an appropriate multiple of one "heavy bomber" under the 1,320 limit, depending upon the agreed maximum.

As it now stands, if the U.S. maintains 550 Minuteman III launchers plus its 496 Poseidon launch tubes, and were to deploy its planned 168 Trident tubes, this would total 1,214 MIRVed missile launchers. This number would exceed the 1,200 limit on MIRVed missile launchers. Therefore, unless there is a delay in the Trident program, the United States will, in any case, have to phase out a small number of Poseidon or Minuteman III launchers. If the U.S. proposes to deploy more than 120 ALCM-carrying planes, it will have to phase out additional Poseidon or Minuteman III launchers in order to stay within the 1,320 limit. It is uncertain that the Navy would recommend phasing out Poseidons, or the Air Force the Minutemen III. Even if the deployment of 120 ALCM-carrying aircraft is assumed, it would be unlikely that more than approximately 50 percent would be on continuous alert, or that more than approximately 90 percent could be brought to readiness under conditions calling for fully generated strategic forces.

The Soviet Union faces a much simpler problem. The U.S. has no substantial air defenses, and the Soviet Backfire is not to be counted under any of the proposed limits. Even if Backfire production is limited to current production rates, the number deployed will grow to a significant total. These bombers can be dispersed to a larger number of fields than can U.S. B-52s, thus enhancing their chances of surviving an initial exchange. In view of the limited American defenses, Backfire-carried Cruise missiles would not need to have a range greater than 600 kilometers. If the Soviets exploit their current technology, they could deploy a significant number of such short-range ALCMs on Backfires prior to 1985. The potential of the Backfire to survive the initial exchanges of a nuclear war, coupled with its capability to penetrate the very limited U.S. defenses, would contribute significantly to a greater possibility of Soviet domination of the subsequent phases of such a war.

Whether the American FB-111H (which is 40 percent the size of the Backfire) can penetrate depends, among other things, on the ability of U.S. tankers to survive in sufficient numbers to provide the required multiple inflight refuelings of the FB-111Hs. If the FB-111H were to carry ALCMs with a range greater than 600 kilometers, they would have to be counted under both the 1,320 ceiling and the 1,200 ceiling.

THE DEFINITION AND VERIFICATION PROBLEMS

It is impossible to verify compliance unless what is to be limited and the nature of the limitation have been clearly defined, and the definition agreed upon in depth between the parties.

As can be seen from the current state of the SALT negotiations, difficult problems in definition are present. It has, for example, proven to be conceptually difficult to define—not merely to negotiate—what constitutes the range of a Cruise missile and how it is to be measured. To turn to another difficult issue, what is the permitted production rate of Backfire bombers? Presumably it is the current rate; the Soviet side will not reveal what that is, but it is reported that the U.S. estimates the rate to be approximately forty per year. What is the permitted "useful payload" of a "small" missile—i.e., beyond what number of pounds of useful payload should a missile be classed as a Modern Large Ballistic Missile (MLBM)? Apparently it is the "throw-weight" of an SS-19—i.e, the maximum useful payload an SS-19-type missile booster has put, or can put, into an intercontinental trajectory. The Soviets, however, will not define "type," will not tell the U.S. how they measure useful payload, and will not reveal what they assess to be the useful payload of an SS-19. Definitional problems extend to other issues, as well.

Even where the limitations are clearly defined, compliance is in many cases difficult to verify. Regardless of how precisely "range" is defined, how can one side verify the range of the other side's Cruise missile? How can the parties to an agreement distinguish an ALCM from a Ground-Launched Cruise Missile (GLCM) or a Submarine-Launched Cruise Missile (SLCM), or assure that an ALCM cannot be launched from a sea- or land-based launcher? How can it be determined whether a Cruise missile is conventionally armed or nuclear armed? How can it be determined that a new missile having the throw-weight of an SS-19 and carrying a bus similar to an SS-19 bus, but with a single RV, is not capable of being deployed as a MIRVed missile? How can it be determined that a missile tested both from land-based launchers and from SLBM submarines is in fact an SLBM and cannot be used as an ICBM? How can it be determined that retired missiles, missiles taken out of retired launchers, or extra, newly produced missiles, are not being stockpiled to be available for relatively prompt deployment on soft pads or for reload in surviving launchers?

In many instances unambiguous verification of the SALT II limitations will not be possible. The arms control community, for this reason, now uses the phrase "adequately verifiable." It is correct that "verifiability" is not an absolute requirement; it is, rather, a means toward the end of a good agreement. A wholly verifiable bad agreement would still be a bad agreement. If those provisions of an agreement which are strategically significant to the U.S. are adequately verifiable, the agreement might be a good agreement, even if its less important provisions are not confidently verifiable. The difficulty, however, rests in determining which provisions are "strategically significant" and what is meant by the word "adequate." Both phrases lend themselves to subjective judgments. If one assumes that no capabilities beyond those required for a "minimum deterrent" are significant, then none of the SALT II limitations are "strategically significant."

THE ACTIVE AND CIVIL DEFENSE
ASPECTS OF THE PROBLEM

The United States has over the last twenty years phased out most of its continental air defense capabilities. The Congress has forced the virtual deactivation of the U.S. ABM defenses permitted under the ABM treaty. In the mid-1960s the U.S. Navy was told that it was not to ask for equipment, men, or funds for the purpose of developing Antisubmarine Warfare (ASW) capabilities designed to attack Soviet SLBMs; as far as it is known that order has never been rescinded.

The U.S.S.R. has persistently put relatively more emphasis on active defensive capabilities than has the United States. The Soviet Union has devoted a truly enormous effort to air defenses. It has deployed 12,000 surface-to-air missile launchers and approximately 2,700 interceptor fighters. It has deployed thousands of inter-netted air defense radars and ground-control-interceptor centers. The Soviets are apparently ready to deploy a new high capability mobile phased-array radar/missile system called the SAX-10. It has recently been reported that the SAX-10 is being deployed on surface ships, thus affording the Soviets the beginnings of a capability to deploy a forward barrier defense against U.S. bomber aircraft.

The Soviet Union has maintained and somewhat improved those ABM capabilities it had earlier deployed in the Moscow area. It is significantly increasing the capabilities of its phased-array ABM "early warning" radars around the periphery of the U.S.S.R. This is permitted under the ABM Treaty on the assumption that, in the event of war, such a network, being close to the periphery, could be destroyed. It is also assumed that the even more powerful radars in the Moscow area could, with greater effort, be destroyed. The large Soviet phased-array radar deployments, when coupled with the development of a transportable phased ABM radar and high acceleration interceptor combination, could, however, give the U.S.S.R. a reasonably rapid break-out toward an important "damage limiting" ABM capability, particularly against U.S. SLBM RVs.

Even more important are the civil defense aspects of the problem. Many observers who have carefully studied the problem concur that a well executed civil defense program—to evacuate most of the population of Moscow and Leningrad would take several days—can reduce fatalities by a factor of five to ten and can substantially reduce industrial damage and the time necessary for economic recovery. There is now little doubt that the Soviet Union is working on civil defense much harder than was realized as recently as two years ago.

It was recently suggested that the Executive Branch would request an expansion of the U.S. civil defense program to include work to enable more rapid evacuation of the American urban population in the event of a crisis. Approval of such a program could be of major importance. It should be noted, however, that, even if that suggestion had proven correct, after such expansion the American program would have cost about one-tenth of what the Executive Branch estimates the Soviets are spending on civil defense.

THE NUMBER AND HARDNESS OF TARGETS PROBLEM

The potential effectiveness of offensive nuclear forces should be judged in connection with the target structure these forces might be called upon to strike. From the standpoint of the military outcome of war, were deterrence to fail, the most important targets are hard targets (silos; launch control facilities; command, control, and communication bunkers; nuclear storage facilities; etc.). It is because of their strategic significance that such targets have been hardened. The list of Soviet hard targets is larger than the American list, and the Soviet targets are generally harder. Additionally, the Soviet list is growing while the American is not. The Soviets will, by the mid-1980s, have twice as many hard targets as the United States, and on the average these targets will be twice as hard.

Against soft targets the important criteria are soft target (area) potential, i.e., Equivalent Megatonnage (EMT), number of warheads, and the relative effectiveness of the civil defense measures on the two sides.

THE BREAK-OUT PROBLEM

The essential effort in the ABM Treaty negotiation was to assure that neither side could break-out of the agreement and thereafter rapidly deploy a significant ABM defense. For this reason, the main emphasis was placed on preventing the deployment of a widespread ABM-capable radar network, the element requiring the longest lead time.

In the early SALT II negotiations the break-out problem with respect to offensive systems was given much attention by the U.S. side. This effort has had to be put to one side in the interest of negotiability, resulting in provisions that leave rapid break-out by the Soviet Union entirely feasible. The proposed provisions designed to limit Soviet ability to reload their silos, for example, cannot be counted on to be effective for more than hours or, at most, days. The proposed SALT agreements appear to involve such phrases as "Cruise missiles can be carried only by heavy bombers." Those persons who have actually worked on and designed Cruise missiles say that any bomber with hard points on its wings can rapidly be converted to carry Cruise missiles and that any Cruise missile operable from a plane can rapidly be adapted for launching from ground- or sea-based launchers.

There seems to be no concern with the potential conversion to a damage-limiting ABM role of new Soviet air defense systems, designed to counter the U.S. Short-Range Attack Missiles (SRAMs)/Cruise missiles.

THE COMMAND, CONTROL, COMMUNICATION, AND PRE- AND POST-ATTACK INTELLIGENCE PROBLEM

Second strike deterrent forces will fail in their purpose if responsible civil authority is not able effectively to command and control these forces. This requires that responsible civil authority survive an attack, have time for a considered and intelligent decision, and be able to communicate with those in immediate control of the launching of surviving forces.

For these decisions to be intelligent and effective, a continuing flow of information covering both the status of U.S. forces and those of the enemy is essential.

Neither those individuals in the Executive Branch nor those outside it have confidence in the current status of American Command, Control, Communication, and Intelligence (C^3 + I). In fact, improving the effectiveness and survivability of C^3 + I is accorded the highest priority by most analysts of the U.S. strategic posture. There is little doubt that the Soviet Union has invested a vastly greater effort than has the U.S. in the development of redundant and survivable C^3 + I systems capable of enduring, if necessary, through a protracted nuclear war. The Soviets have also been developing antisatellite and other capabilities which could deny the U.S. pre- and post-attack intelligence.

It was hoped that the SALT II provision obligating each side not to interfere with the other side's national technical means of verification would give useful protection to U.S. pre-attack technical intelligence capabilities. With the ambiguous resolution of the test range telemetry encryption problem, however, much of America's technical intelligence capability becomes dependent on unilateral Soviet decisions.

Finally, the diminishing survivability and endurance potential of American strategic forces which can be expected during the Treaty period sharpen the need for improved U.S. post-attack C^3 + I.

THE RELATION OF THE STRATEGIC NUCLEAR BALANCE TO THE CONVENTIONAL AND NUCLEAR THEATER BALANCE

At all times since World War II the Soviet Union has had superior non-nuclear forces on the European central front and on its northern and southern flanks. This has, in part, been due to geography, with the U.S.S.R.

enjoying the central position and interior lines, and, in part, to the greater effort, as compared to NATO, that has been made by the Soviet Union and the Warsaw Pact.

In the years up to the early 1950s this Soviet advantage was offset by the U.S. nuclear monopoly. In later years the U.S. conventional deficiency was in large measure offset by U.S. superiority in theater nuclear weapons. Today that theater nuclear superiority has disappeared, and in order to maintain a theater balance it has proved necessary to assign a number of Poseidon submarines to cover targets of interest to NATO. It has been estimated that in comparison with the U.S. the Soviet Union has two to three times as many theater nuclear weapons, with six times the area destructive potential, ten times the throw-weight, and twenty-five times the megatonnage. As the Soviets deploy increasing numbers of SS-20 MIRVed missiles, Backfires, and other high performance theater bombers, it will become increasingly difficult to maintain a theater nuclear balance. In addition to the theater nuclear imbalance, the substantial and one-sided Saret Pact chemical warfare capabilities must be considered. More and more of the surviving U.S. strategic nuclear forces will be called upon for assignment to offset theater imbalances. This consideration is rarely taken into account when the strategic nuclear balance is being examined; it should be, however.

Moreover, the SALT II agreements could have a serious negative effect upon the evolution of the conventional balance. The European NATO countries have hoped to exploit Cruise missile technology in its theater conventional weapon applications. A SALT accord that limited armed Cruise missiles with a range greater than 600 kilometers would favor the Soviet side. It would support the erroneous Soviet claim that nuclear ballistic missiles deployed in the Soviet Union for peripheral area missions, with medium or inter-

mediate ranges, which under SALT II can be up to
5,500 kilometers, are not "strategic," while Cruise
missiles deployed in NATO Europe, if over 600 kilometers in range, whether nuclear or conventionally armed,
are "strategic."

In specific terms, the SALT II agreements—particularly if there is acceptance of the Soviet position
that conventionally armed as well as nuclear armed
Cruise missiles are to be limited—may, as a result of
limitations on the transfer of weapons, components, or
technical information relating to weapons restricted by
the SALT Treaty, prevent the U.S. from transferring
technology important to the conventional defense of
Europe, as well as prohibit the deployment by the U.S.
of conventionally armed Cruise missiles with ranges
greater than 600 kilometers. These agreements could
also result in the limiting of the U.S. Navy to Cruise
missiles less than 600 kilometers in range; countries not
party to the agreements would of course not be
confined in this manner, and could then significantly
out-range the U.S. Navy.

THE IMPACT OF THE AGREEMENT UPON THE ABILITY OF THE UNITED STATES TO REVERSE CURRENT TRENDS

The Vladivostok Accord did not restrict the U.S.S.R.
from deploying those new weapon systems it planned to
deploy, but neither did it restrict the U.S. from
deploying those weapon systems necessary to maintain
stability and rough equivalence. It did not restrict the
ability of the United States to deploy the B-1; the
Minuteman III and the MX missiles in a survivable
deployment mode; Trident II; ALCMs, GLCMs, and
SLCMs of any range; continental air defenses; more
durable and reliable command and control; or enhanced
civil defense preparations. U.S. program decisions and

delays in making decisions since Vladivostok, combined with the terms of the probable SALT II agreements, now make it difficult, if not impossible, for the U.S. to maintain crisis stability and rough equivalence.

It is argued by some observers that the restrictions in the agreements, as they apply to the United States, are of little significance; they do not keep the U.S. from doing anything it now should or would want to do during the period of the agreements. The accuracy or falsehood of this assertion depends in large measure on whether or not the agreements permit the deployment of a multiple verticle protective structure system (MVPS). Under this concept the U.S. would construct a large number of vertical protective shelters or silos, each capable of holding a cannister containing an ICBM (a Minuteman III or a follow-on missile such as the MX) and its launch mechanism or, alternatively, a cannister which would contain no missile or launch mechanism but which would be indistinguishable from those that did. The U.S. is reported to have told the Soviets that it considered such a system to be permitted under the proposed Treaty. The Soviet side is reported to have expressed its most serious reservations about any such interpretation. If it is decided that a MVPS deployment is permitted, it is conceivable that the U.S. could deploy such a system rapidly enough to maintain crisis stability. If such a decision is not reached—which appears most likely since the system is not a truly mobile system (it is transportable, not mobile)—there does not appear to be any feasible, alternate way to maintain crisis stability within the next decade or more.

Under the currently most likely provisions of a SALT II accord, it is difficult, if not impossible, to see how the U.S. can reverse recent adverse trends in the military balance. Beginning in the early to mid-1980s, if deterrence fails the U.S. would have to rely on an ICBM force which will be useful only if the President decides to launch it from under an attack in the few minutes he may have available to do so; a bomber force capable of enduring no more than a few hours, if not used earlier; and an SLBM force at-sea of less than twenty-five boats, each boat constituting 4 percent of U.S. "enduring" deterrent power and thus worth enormous Soviet efforts to negate.

THE SITUATION IN THE ABSENCE OF AN AGREEMENT

The proponents of ratification of the accords emphasize that whereas the U.S.S.R. now has some 2,500 strategic launchers, under SALT II it will have to reduce these to 2,400 some months after the agreements enter into force and to 2,250 some three years thereafter. These persons assert that in the absence of an agreement, the Soviet side may not make any such reductions and may well add some 400, or even more, new strategic launchers to the number which would be permitted under SALT II.

Past experience, however, indicates that this is unlikely. The most careful student of previous Soviet defense budgets and programs, William T. Lee, argues that he can identify little if any modification in the general magnitude of Soviet defense budgets, and therefore of defense programs, in response to international events or changes in U.S. programs. Whereas it is generally said that the increased Soviet emphasis on expanding its intercontinental strategic capabilities was in direct response to the Cuban missile crisis, Lee finds no evidence that this is so. The Soviet five-year planning process is so interrelated and complex that any changes beyond marginal adjustments are extremely disruptive and, in the past, have rarely occurred. Lee also notes the difficulty the Soviets would have in increasing the percentage of their GNP devoted to defense, which according to his estimates has now risen to approximately 18 percent. Nevertheless, the possibility cannot be excluded that the Soviet side, in the absence of SALT II, would not decrease the number of its strategic launchers to 2,250 and would, instead, increase them.

It should be noted, however, that the 300 launchers the Soviets are expected to phase out to reach 2,250 are obsolete ICBMs and SLBMs which add little to Soviet overall capabilities. Their presently programmed forces, largely composed of new missiles, will provide them with such an excess of MIRVed hard target kill capability, unMIRVed megatonnage, and RVs needed for target coverage, that it is hard to see what strategic benefit they would gain from more of the same. Increased intermediate range systems to cover requirements against China are not limited by SALT.

It is now anticipated that as the U.S.S.R. completes its deployment of new ICBMs and SLBMs the Soviets will concentrate more heavily on adding to their defensive capabilities, for this is where the principal gaps in their warmaking potential now lie. In particular, they are expected to add more attack submarines designed for an ASW role and aircraft with improved look-down/ shoot-down radar capabilities, and to deploy improved antiaircraft systems such as their SAX-10 mobile antiaircraft batteries, etc. For the Soviet Union to shift resources back to offensive forces from a contemplated strengthening of its defenses may not be disadvantageous to the United States.

The more important question centers around what the United States can be expected to do under the SALT II agreements—and in the absence of such agreements—to reverse currently unfavorable strategic nuclear trends.

THE QUESTION OF STRATEGY

The question of what strategy the U.S. should follow

if deterrence were to fail, and the issue of the relationship of strategy to deterrence, are fundamental to the debate concerning SALT II and concerning the U.S. strategic nuclear program.

Some analysts start from the assumption that a nuclear war is "unthinkable." According to this line of thinking, those persons who do think about nuclear war must be Dr. Strangeloves; deterrence has nothing to do with the military strategy either side intends to follow in the event deterrence were to fail; and, regardless of strategy and of the probable balance of the initially surviving and then enduring nuclear forces, there could be no meaningful winner or loser in a nuclear war.

Other observers believe that a nuclear war is thinkable and that the United States can best avoid a nuclear war, while preserving its independence and honor, by thinking seriously about nuclear war and taking prudent and timely action to forestall it. In this view, the quality of deterrence is importantly affected by the strategy the U.S. intends to follow and could effectively implement if deterrence were to fail. These persons question the wisdom and credibility of a so-called minimum deterrence strategy, under which deterrence would depend on the ability and will of the U.S. to launch, in response to a Soviet attack, some limited number of warheads against Soviet cities and industry, which are protected by extensive active and passive defenses. This strategy seems to ignore the fact that the remaining U.S. population and industry would then be defenseless against ten thousand megatons or more of a Soviet third and fourth strike capability.

Few analysts now overtly support the minimum deterrence approach; they are more apt to describe their position with such phrases as "sufficiency" or "flexibility." This leads to the question: how much of what is enough? That judgment in turn must rest importantly upon the relative emphasis placed on the counterforce and the countervalue aspects of nuclear strategy.

Neither of these aspects can be ignored. If the U.S. counterforce capabilities which survived an initial Soviet strike were sufficient to out-fight Soviet residual forces, while other U.S. forces were capable of surviving and enduring to hold Soviet population and industry in reciprocal danger to American population and industry, the quality of deterrence would be high, since the Soviets would know the U.S. was in a position to implement a credible military strategy in the event deterrence were to fail.

If U.S. strategy were restricted to an immediate revenge attack on, for instance, the 200 largest Soviet cities, the military forces required to support such a strategy would be relatively small. Such a strategy, however, would lead to instability in a crisis and would be suicidal if implemented, vastly more destructive to the U.S. than to the Soviet Union, and militarily hopeless. One could, therefore, have only limited confidence in deterrence based upon an implied determination to execute such a strategy to defend vital U.S. interests.

Those that claim that the U.S. is stronger than the Soviet Union now and will continue to be so during our lifetimes, more or less regardless of what the U.S. does, must equate forces designed to support such a minimum deterrence strategy with superiority.

THE CONTINUING NEGOTIATION PROBLEM

It has been characteristic of the SALT negotiation process that the U.S. Executive Branch in justifying existing agreements has stressed its hope that the deficiencies in these accords will be corrected in future agreements. This argument characterized the justification of the SALT I Interim Agreement. That accord specified that its terms were not to prejudice in any way the scope or the terms of the long term comprehensive agreement contemplated for its replacement, the negotiation of which both sides had agreed should begin immediately after entry into force of the Interim Agreement. Despite the best efforts of the U.S. side, however, the terms of the Interim Agreement have, in fact, prejudiced the terms of SALT II. The nature of the continuing programs of the two sides and the political and psychological pressures on the U.S. made it difficult to achieve any other result.

It is contemplated that SALT III negotiations will begin shortly after SALT II is ratified and enters into force. Two hurdles must be met by the U.S. negotiators during those talks: the expiration of the Protocol around January 1, 1982, and the expiration of the Treaty at the end of 1985. It is likely that the negotiations will be concerned with both subjects, and that the Soviet side will press for the extension of those provisions of the Protocol which they would have preferred to see in the Treaty. This pressure will then be linked to the SALT III treaty negotiation. The question of whether the U.S. can expect to prevail with respect to its hopes for SALT III will largely depend on the relative bargaining positions of the two sides during the negotiations. The evolution of the relative strength of the two sides in the strategic nuclear arena is almost certain to be negative with respect to the U.S. position during the entire period prior to expiration of the SALT II Treaty. If the MX and Trident II versions of the "largely-common missile" are then almost ready for initial operational deployment, this could have a favorable bearing on the negotiations. The impending deployment of the MX version could, however, be destabilizing if a basing mode capable of assuring its survivability and endurance were not concurrently available.

If the SALT II Treaty were to expire in 1985 without replacement and without a survivable and durable U.S. ICBM component, the U.S. could face unprecedented dangers. The U.S. would then be forced to take seriously both the then-existing Soviet nuclear strategic superiority and a superior Soviet break-out potential. To avoid these risks, the U.S. would be under pressure to agree to a SALT III agreement even less favorable than SALT II, rather than hold out for a more favorable accord.

THE POLITICAL AND DIPLOMATIC CONSEQUENCES OF A SHIFT IN THE STRATEGIC NUCLEAR BALANCE

Some proponents of the SALT accords, rather than taking exception to the main thrust of the analysis contained in the preceding sections, argue a different series of points along the following lines:

a) The March 1977 comprehensive proposal of the United States leaned over backward in attempting to be fair to the Soviet Union. It offered the Soviets complete assurance against any significant counterforce threat from the United States, while not assuring comparable protection for the U.S.

b) That proposal proved wholly unacceptable to the U.S.S.R., and any proposal which would in fact assure stability and rough equivalence at lower levels of nuclear armaments would be even more unnegotiable.

c) For the U.S. to insist on such an equitable agreement would assure that there would be no success, at least in the next few years, in negotiating a SALT II set of agreements. Such a delay would risk a breakdown of detente.

d) Rather than risk such a breakdown, it is wiser to negotiate the best deal that can now be attained, preserve at least the outward forms of detente, and open the way to follow-on negotiations to seek a better deal in the future.

e) And, in any case—so this argument goes—a deterioration in the state of the strategic nuclear balance will have no adverse political or diplomatic consequences.

To some of those persons who lived through the Berlin crisis in 1961, the Cuban crisis in 1962, or the Middle East crisis in 1973, the last and key judgment in this chain of reasoning—that an adverse shift in the strategic nuclear balance will have no political or diplomatic consequences—comes as a shock. In the Berlin crisis of 1961 the U.S. theater position was clearly unfavorable; the U.S. relied entirely on its strategic nuclear superiority to face down Chairman Khrushchev's ultimatum. In Cuba, the Soviet Union faced a position of both theater inferiority and strategic inferiority; the Soviets withdrew the missiles they were deploying. In the 1973 Middle East crisis, the theater and the strategic nuclear strengths were more balanced; both sides compromised.

It is hard to see what factors in the future are apt to disconnect international politics and diplomacy from a consideration of the underlying real power balances. The nuclear balance is only one element in the overall power balance—but in the Soviet view, it is the fulcrum upon which rest all other levels of influence: military, economic, and political. How confident can the United States be that there is not at least a measure of validity to that viewpoint?

C. TABLES AND FIGURES

Table 1

THE BALANCE IN NUMBERS OF STRATEGIC NUCLEAR LAUNCH VEHICLES (SNLVs)

	1977		Consistent with SALT II Proposals 1982		1985	
	U.S.	S.U.	U.S.	S.U.	U.S.	S.U.
ICBMs						
— MIRV	550	164	550	820	536	820
— Non-MIRV	504	1,392	504	390	504	360
Total	1,054	1,556	1,054	1,210	1,040	1,180
SLBMs						
— MIRV	496	28	640	308	664	356
— Non-MIRV	160	764	160	668	80	620
Total	656	792	800	976	744	976
Heavy Bombers						
	346	150	331 Non-ALCM		226 Non-ALCM	
			15 ALCM	64	120 ALCM	90
Total SNDVs	2,056	2,498	2,200	2,250	2,130	2,246

NOTE: This table does not include allowances for FB-111 and Backfire aircraft on the U.S. and Soviet sides, respectively. Additionally, no allowances for operational launchers at test ranges on either side are included in this table.

Table 2

THE BALANCE IN NUMBERS OF WARHEADS

	1977		Consistent with SALT II Proposals 1982		1985	
	U.S.	S.U.	U.S.	S.U.	U.S.	S.U.
ICBMs						
— MIRV	1,650	620	1,650	5,752	1,608	5,752
— Non-MIRV	504	1,872	504	680	504	480
Total	2,154	2,492	2,154	6,432	2,112	6,232
SLBMs						
— MIRV	3,328	84	5,120	888 (2,912)	5,312	1,068 (3,752)
— Non-MIRV	480	764	480	704	240	620
Total	3,808	848	5,600	1,592 (3,616)	5,552	1,688 (4,372)
Heavy Bombers (ALCMs, SRAMs, Gravity Bombs)						
Total	2,564	170	2,836	300	4,484	350
Total Warheads	8,526	3,510	10,590	8,324 (10,348)	12,148	8,270 (10,954)

( ) —   Numbers in parentheses assume payload for SS-N-18 and Typhoon of 7 and 14 RVs, respectively. Numbers not in parentheses assume 3 RVs on each of larger megatonnage.

NOTE: This table does not include allowances for FB-111 and Backfire aircraft on the U.S. and Soviet sides, respectively. Additionally, no allowances for operational launchers at test ranges on either side are included in this table.

Table 3

THE BALANCE IN HARD TARGET KILL POTENTIAL — CMP* ($nY^{2/3}/CEP^2$)

	1977		Consistent with SALT II Proposals 1982		1985	
	U.S.	S.U.	U.S.	S.U.	U.S.	S.U.
Assumed CEP** **of MIRVed ICBMs** **in feet**	600	1,200	600	900	600	600
ICBMs						
— MIRV	22,239	16,999	42,232	273,904	41,004	410,856
— Non-MIRV	8,939	24,440	8,939	29,425	8,939	128,048
Total	31,178	41,439	51,171	303,329	49,943	538,904
SLBMs						
— MIRV	8,576	519	12,160	7,472 (8,761)	12,667	12,192 (16,104)
— Non-MIRV	317	4,011	317	3,244	159	5,578
Total	8,893	4,530	12,477	10,716 (12,005)	12,826	17,770 (21,682)
Heavy Bombers (ALCMs, SRAMs, Gravity Bombs) **[Assumed CEP of U.S. ALCMs-300 ft.]**						
Total	56,163	12,400	96,127	20,000	338,263 [84,565] †	35,000
Total CMP	96,234	58,369	159,775	334,045 (335,334)	401,032 [147,334]	591,674 †(595,586)

*CMP = Countermilitary Potential

**CEP = Circular Error Probable

†If effective CEP against hard targets of 600 feet is assumed, the units of hard target kill capability of ALCMs are reduced by a factor of 4.

( ) — Numbers in parentheses assume payload for SS-N-18 and Typhoon of 7 and 14 RVs, respectively. Numbers not in parentheses assume 3 RVs on each of larger megatonnage.

NOTE: This table does not include allowances for FB-111 and Back-fire aircraft on the U.S. and Soviet sides, respectively. Additionally, no allowances for operational launchers at test ranges on either side are included in this table.

Table 4

THE BALANCE IN AREA DESTRUCTION POTENTIAL — EMT* ($nY^{2/3}$)

	1977		Consistent with SALT II Proposals 1982		1985	
	U.S.	S.U.	U.S.	S.U.	U.S.	S.U.
ICBMs						
— MIRV	512	620	726	5,752	694	5,752
— Non-MIRV	730	4,258	730	1,086	730	1,845
Total	1,242	4,878	1,456	6,838	1,424	7,597
SLBMs						
— MIRV	434	84	787	559 (612)	819	672 (788)
— Non-MIRV	178	764	178	668	89	584
Total	612	848	965	1,227 (1,280)	908	1,256 (1,372)
Heavy Bombers (ALCMs, SRAMs, Gravity Bombs)						
Total	1,785	350	1,833	425	2,049	497
Total Area Destruction	3,639	6,076	4,254	8,490 (8,543)	4,381	9,350 (9,466)

( ) — Numbers in parentheses assume payload for SS-N-18 and Typhoon of 7 and 14 RVs, respectively. Numbers not in parentheses assume 3 RVs on each of larger megatonnage.

NOTE: This table does not include allowances for FB-111 and Backfire aircraft on the U.S. and Soviet sides, respectively. Additionally, no allowances for operational launchers at test ranges on either side are included in this table.

*EMT = Equivalent Megatonnage

Table 5

THE BALANCE IN MEGATONNAGE

	1977		Consistent with SALT II Proposals 1982		1985	
	U.S.	S.U.	U.S.	S.U.	U.S.	S.U.
ICBMs						
– MIRV	280	620	462	5,752	450	5,752
– Non-MIRV	1,026	5,565	1,026	1,950	1,026	4,593
Total	1,306	6,185	1,488	7,702	1,476	10,345
SLBMs						
– MIRV	197	42	320	444	333	534
				(291)		(375)
– Non-MIRV	110	764	110	668	55	600
Total	307	806	430	1,112	388	1,134
				(959)		(975)
Heavy Bombers (ALCMs, SRAMs, Gravity Bombs)						
Total	1,274	500	1,291	213	1,404	300
Total Megatonnage	2,887	7,491	3,209	9,027	3,268	11,779
				(8,874)		(11,620)

( ) –   Numbers in parentheses assume payload for SS-N-18 and Typhoon of 7 and 14 RVs, respectively. Numbers not in parentheses assume 3 RVs on each of larger megatonnage.

NOTE: This table does not include allowances for FB-111 and Backfire aircraft on the U.S. and Soviet sides, respectively. Additionally, no allowances for operational launchers at test ranges on either side are included in this table.

Table 6

THE BALANCE IN THROW-WEIGHT (Millions of pounds)

	1977 U.S.	1977 S.U.	Consistent with SALT II Proposals 1982 U.S.	1982 S.U.	1985 U.S.	1985 S.U.
ICBMs						
– MIRV	1.3	1.6	1.3	8.8	1.3	9.8
– Non-MIRV	1.2	6.1	1.2	1.3	1.2	2.2
Total	2.5	7.7	2.5	10.1	2.5	12.0
SLBMs						
– MIRV	1.6	0.1	2.1	1.0	2.1	1.3
– Non-MIRV	0.2	1.2	.2	1.1	0.1	1.1
Total	1.8	1.3	2.3	2.1	2.2	2.4
Heavy Bombers	4.0	1.7	3.5	0.7	3.5	1.0
Total T.W. (M/lbs)	8.3	10.7	8.3	12.9	8.2	15.4

NOTE: This table does not include allowances for FB-111 and Backfire aircraft on the U.S. and Soviet sides, respectively. Additionally, no allowance for operational launchers at test ranges
on either side are included in this table.

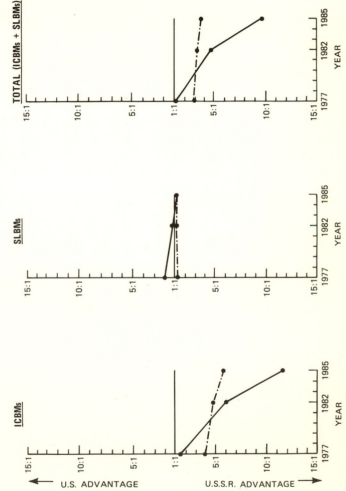

FIGURE 1. THE BALANCE — CONSEQUENCES OF CURRENT SALT PROPOSALS
Time Urgent Counter-Military and Soft Target Destruction Potential

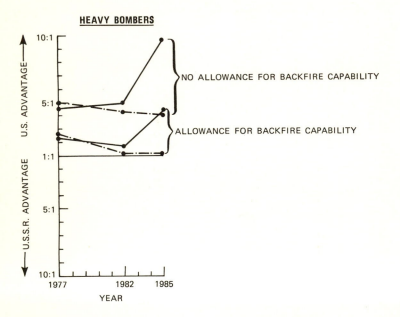

FIGURE 2.　THE BALANCE — CONSEQUENCES OF CURRENT SALT PROPOSALS
Delayed Counter-Military and Soft Target Destruction Potential

——————— DELAYED COUNTER-MILITARY POTENTIAL
—·——·——·— DELAYED SOFT AREA TARGET DESTRUCTION POTENTIAL (EMT)

HEAVY BOMBERS

NO ALLOWANCE FOR BACKFIRE CAPABILITY

ALLOWANCE FOR BACKFIRE CAPABILITY

U.S. ADVANTAGE

U.S.S.R. ADVANTAGE

YEAR

THIS FIGURE ASSUMES THE U.S. PROGRESSIVELY EQUIPS 120 B-52s EACH WITH
20 ALCMs OF HIGH ACCURACY. IT INCLUDES NO ALLOWANCE FOR THE POTENTIAL
OF AIR DEFENSES. IT ALSO INCLUDES NO ALLOWANCE FOR THE POSSIBLE DEPLOYMENT
ON BACKFIRE OF CRUISE MISSILES WITH LESS THAN 600 KM RANGE THAT INCORPORATES
THE TECHNOLOGY OF CURRENT SOVIET DEVELOPMENTAL PROGRAMS.

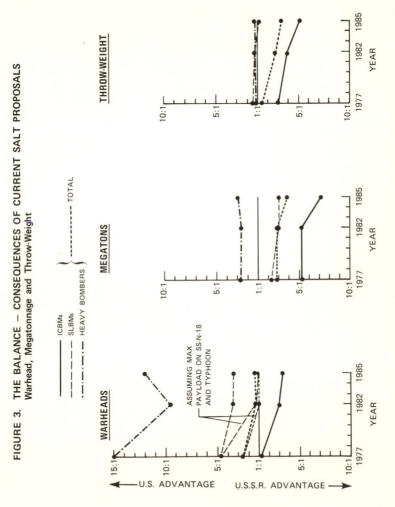

FIGURE 3. THE BALANCE — CONSEQUENCES OF CURRENT SALT PROPOSALS
Warhead, Megatonnage and Throw-Weight

THIS FIGURE DOES NOT INCLUDE ALLOWANCES FOR BACKFIRE CAPABILITY

TABLE 7

**COMPARISON OF CALCULATIONS IN FIGURES 1, 2, & 3
WITH SEC DEF BROWN'S FIGURES IN FY 1978
BUDGET AMENDMENT TESTIMONY, TABLE 2**

Static Measures of Strategic Balance
(U.S. as % of Soviet)

	BROWN'S		FIGURES 1, 2, & 3	
	1977	1986 (B-52/CM)	1977	1985 (B-52/CM)
WARHEADS	240%	126%	249%	149%
MEGATONS	35%	25%	36%	27%
THROW-WEIGHT	75%	48%	68%	47%
COUNTER-MILITARY POTENTIAL	160%	67%	165%	67%

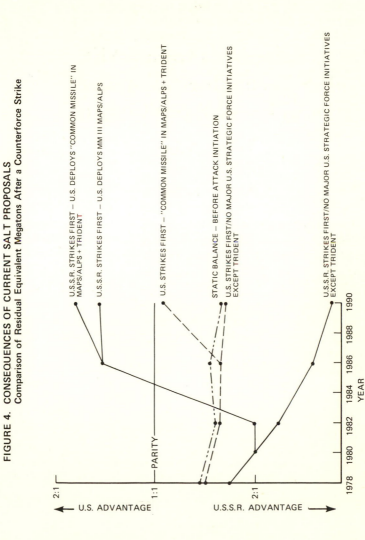

FIGURE 4. CONSEQUENCES OF CURRENT SALT PROPOSALS
Comparison of Residual Equivalent Megatons After a Counterforce Strike

THIS FIGURE DOES NOT INCLUDE ALLOWANCES FOR BACKFIRE CAPABILITY

3

Safeguards from SALT: U.S. Technological Strategy in an Era of Arms Control

Francis X. Kane

INTRODUCTION

Ardent proponents of arms reductions have criticized the SALT process as being the codifier of the "Arms Race" and the justification for continuing "Arms Buildups." It is indeed the case that in ratifying the SALT I Treaty and Agreement of 1972, the U.S. Congress approved, as a direct outgrowth of those accords, a set of "safeguards"* in the form of funded programs perceived as necessary for the maintenance of U.S. security.[1]

Even before the negotiations for the SALT II Treaty have been completed, there is growing recognition that

---

*The term "safeguard" has been used in connection with several arms control agreements negotiated with the Soviets, including the ban on testing nuclear weapons, the Anti-Ballistic Missile (ABM) Treaty, and the SALT I Interim Agreement covering strategic delivery vehicles. The term is symptomatic of a basic strategic issue: these measures upon which agreement has been reached are not adequate for ensuring U.S. security. Consequently, these agreements must be accompanied by funded defense programs which provide "safeguards" against the deficiencies in the accords and against the possibility of treaty failure or abrogation. [There was also a specific Ballistic Missile Defense Program called the Safeguard; it was terminated after the SALT I agreements were reached.]

the United States will not reach one of the principal goals it has sought through the accord, for the Soviet threat to the American land-based Intercontinental Ballistic Missile (ICBM) force will continue to grow even during the new Treaty period. Once again, therefore, the U.S. must have a program of "safeguards" to protect its security against deficiencies in the outcome of the SALT process. Why is this so, and what must the U.S. do?

The United States has two dominant goals in the SALT negotiations: to maintain a stable balance of strategic power with the Soviets and to negotiate reductions in the level of strategic forces.[2] The SALT I Treaty and Agreement placed limits on some elements of the strategic forces of both sides. The Vladivostok Agreement defined additional limits, and in the proposed SALT II Treaty there are provisions for numerical reductions. The continuing Soviet arms buildup threatens the balance of strategic power, however, and the U.S. is faced with a potential condition of strategic instability. One of the principal U.S. objectives—the maintenance of strategic/global stability—is therefore not being achieved.

Two geopolitical factors which the U.S. cannot control—the Soviet enmity towards the U.S. and the onrush of technology—contribute crucially to this failure to maintain strategic stability. The U.S. can try to mitigate the former; it must capitalize on the latter. Technology is dynamic, however, making the process of maintaining stability a dynamic process. *The most important step toward the dual U.S. goals expressed in SALT is the implementation of innovative research and development (R&D) programs.*

The advent of the Strategic Arms Limitation Talks and the potential that they will continue for the rest of the century require that the role of the research and development process in U.S. technological strategy be clearly defined and understood. In order to ensure future U.S. security, care must be taken to guard against the potential of an enemy "surge" beyond treaty limits either by the deployment of additional forces or by the acquisition of new systems. In other words, the U.S. must have safeguards to counter Soviet efforts which can lead to new capabilities disturbing to the essential strategic balance. Furthermore, if the United States implements an effective technological strategy it will have the potential for reducing the amount of power deployed on both sides while maintaining dynamic stability.

The key to such stability lies in the existence of surviving strategic forces which can carry out the basic missions under a variety of conditions. At the same time, these forces should not be at such a high level of capability that they pose an overwhelming threat and thus provoke further efforts to increase the number of forces deployed.

It is fundamental to keep in mind, however, that arms negotiations and the arms control process really do not strike at the heart of the matter. Several decades ago the Soviet Union deliberately chose the U.S. as its enemy. For purely ideological reasons, the Soviets picked as their principal adversary a nation which in no way threatened them and which in fact had twice helped to preserve the Soviet regime (with the American Relief Administration at the end of World War I, and during World War II). Since World War II, the U.S. has been a status quo power while taking the defensive against Soviet expansionist aims and efforts. In every major crisis in Soviet affairs (e.g., Hungary and Czechoslovakia), the U.S. has acquiesed to Moscow's hegemony over the countries it seized at the end of World War II. The U.S. is not trying to overthrow the Soviet regime or even force its withdrawal to its national borders. Similarly, the U.S. has not and does not pose an economic threat to the Soviet Union.[3] Nevertheless, there is every indication that Soviet enmity will persist and that the basic security challenge posed by the Soviets will endure. Arms control efforts and arms reductions may mitigate some of the effects of this enmity, but they can in no way eliminate it. The struggle will thus continue, and strategic forces will remain vital to the maintenance of a condition of dynamic stability.

It is to its R&D process and its technological strategy that the U.S. must look for the key to such stability for the coming decades. This essential fact runs counter to the conventional wisdom of the arms control community. Some arms controllers believe that the way to "eliminate the arms race" is to limit R&D. In many ways this view is and has been at the core of the U.S. approach to the SALT efforts. Nearly all the American proposals have aimed at limiting research and development—for example by restricting flight testing or by prohibiting future weapons, such as ballistic missile defenses. Nevertheless, the reality is that such a technological strategy is utopian, for there is no way to limit the technological process. Attempts to use SALT as a tool for limitations on future systems research and development simply shift the area of activity to one of qualitatively improving the performance of current systems.[4] The net effect of such an approach could be technological surprise.

If the United States is faced in the future with technological surprise which could negate the survivability of an element of its strategic offensive forces—for example, a breakthrough in Antisubmarine Warfare (ASW) which would result in the vulnerability of American Submarine-Launched Ballistic Missiles (SLBMs)—it would respond by doing what has been done in years past: dramatically increase the amount of deployed power in one of the other elements of the American strategic force posture. The essence of this technological strategy is to find survivability through increased numbers, but increased numbers mean more deployed weapons. Consequently, this "strength in numbers" strategy runs directly counter to the second U.S. objective, which is to reduce the amount of deployed raw power in the arsenals of both sides. Rather than attaining the goal of arms control, limitations or prohibitions on research and development can thus be self-defeating. The conclusion to be drawn is that the U.S. must capitalize on research and development to attain both of its basic objectives: stability and the reduction of deployed power.

The U.S. program of safeguards should take into account three areas of technology where developments could result in new threats. First of all, qualitative improvements can be made in existing systems, resulting in better performance. The Soviet program to improve their Anti-Ballistic Missile System serves as an example. Under the ABM Treaty both sides agreed to numerical limits on their ABM, but qualitative improvements were not constrained. It has been reported that the Soviet Union is continuing to improve its ABM; there is thus concern that a Soviet "surge" in this area could reduce the effectiveness of U.S. ballistic missiles launched in retaliatory strikes.

The deployment of entirely new systems constitutes a second type of possible "surge." Even though the Soviets are already deploying large numbers of new ICBMs and SLBMs, they are also developing a fifth generation ICBM and a supersonic long-range bomber. These new weapon systems could be fielded within the SALT limitations; but, by replacing older systems, they would improve the performance of the Soviet forces. Alternatively, they could provide the base for a rapid violation of treaty limits, thus greatly increasing the Soviet threat to the United States.

Additionally, there is the realm of new scientific discoveries and their applications to weapon systems. The clearest example presently is the development of high energy and "beam weapon" technology.[5] It is too early to determine where these developments will lead or to know how they will be applied to strategic forces. The U.S. obviously cannot remain ignorant of the potential applications, but must stay abreast of such developments in order to understand their potential strategic impact and to be prepared to respond to any threatening Soviet advance. This is especially important if there is a U.S. reduction in the number of deployed weapons, for such a reduction will necessitate survivable forces which can operate effectively—both as a continuing deterrent and as weapons to be used if the U.S. fails to deter.

Ideally, the American R&D process should embody sufficient options so that the U.S.—because it will be able to mount an effective counteraction to any Soviet advances—will, in a sense, be immune to Soviet breakthroughs. The net result of this approach would be to deter continued R&D on the Soviet side, since it would be clear that the process would in the end lead the Soviets to no advantage over the U.S. In summary, if the United States constructs its R&D program properly, it can enforce stability.

American technological strategy in an arms control environment is only one element of U.S. defense strategy. It must reinforce U.S. negotiating positions and provide options for arms reduction and for safeguards. Future U.S. defense strategy must avoid a recurrence of the present American difficulty, whereby approval of SALT II is justified on the basis that—however problematical the accords may be—the U.S. alternatives without SALT II are worse. The Soviets do not have this problem; their vigorous R&D program has kept their options open, and they have alternatives to SALT. The United States in the future should integrate its security objectives and its strategic programs so as to prevent such an asymmetry from occurring again.[6]

A.PRINCIPLES OF TECHNOLOGICAL STRATEGY

LEAD TIME

The factor of time is vitally important in the maintenance of stability. *Figure 1* presents a theoretical model of the U.S. reaction to a Soviet deployment after the Soviet R&D program is recognized. In comparisons of the weapon system acquisition process on each side, a continuing phenomenon is the mismatch in lead time from system concept to deployment. *Figure 2* illustrates this mismatch as it existed several years ago with respect to ICBMs. The Soviets were able to gain years of time advantage because much of their R&D program was and is invisible to the U.S.

While the United States can observe the Soviet deployment of weapon systems, it has only limited insight into Soviet R&D programs. The first visible indicators of ICBMs, for example, come with the flight tests of the booster and re-entry vehicle and with the construction of the bases. By that stage of the program, the Soviets are only a few years from having the new ICBM in their operational arsenal. (This is shown in the upper part of *Figure 2.*) In previous reactions to the visible evidence of Soviet deployment (Alternative A on *Figure 2*), the U.S. required two to three years to modify its budget and three to five years to develop and field a new system.[7]

Alternative B in *Figure 2* assumes a technological strategy in which there are dynamic programs at various stages of development, especially prototypes of new systems. Given the array of systems, a decision can be made to choose the most appropriate reaction to the perceived Soviet advance and thus restore the strategic balance.

The lead time for acquisition of strategic forces has now increased dramatically and for the U.S. is currently

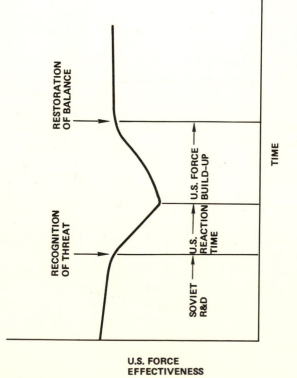

Figure 1.   US Reaction to Soviet Strategic Threat
(Theoretical Model)

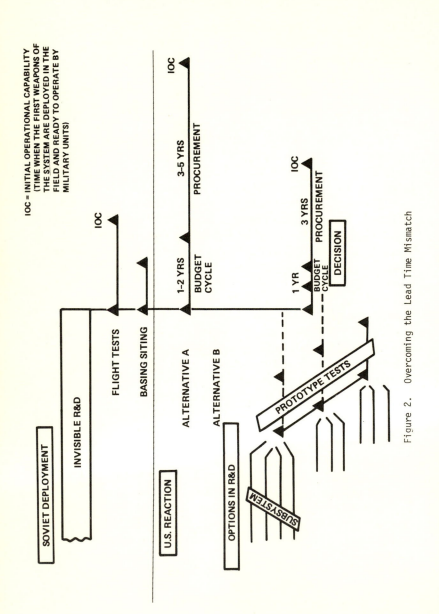

Figure 2.   Overcoming the Lead Time Mismatch

in the realm of ten to twelve years. For other parts of the R&D process, the lead time can be even longer. The satellite program called the Global Positioning System[8], for example, was designed conceptually in the early 1960s but will not be fully operational until the mid- to late 1980s. In this case, therefore, the lead time is over two decades.

The present debate concerning the proper U.S. response to the Soviet threat to American ICBMs illuminates this problem of lead time. Forecasts were made in the early 1960s that technological changes would result in the vulnerability of hard silos. It was difficult, however, to predict when this would occur. Some analysts asserted that the Soviets would not build more than 800 ICBMs.[9] Others argued that the Soviet technology was too primitive to result in a threat in the foreseeable future.[10] More recently, it has become generally accepted that the technical improvements in Soviet weapons are leading to the vulnerability of American ICBMs; it is asserted, however, that operational difficulties and questions make that vulnerability only theoretical until after 1990.[11] Because of these uncertainties, no U.S. program was set forth to cope with the eventual condition of ICBM vulnerability. During the past fifteen years many alternatives to the present Minuteman force have been studied and analyzed. An R&D program is presently being conducted to develop a new missile, the MX, and a new mode of ICBM basing, called the Multiple Protective Structures (MPS) program, is being studied.[12] For several years hopes were pinned on the SALT process as the way to constrain the Soviet force buildup and threat, but there is now almost unanimous acceptance of the fact that SALT will fail to accomplish this aim. Even if the U.S. were to decide now to develop and deploy the MX/MPS, it would be seven to ten years before a significant force would be fielded.

The lack of U.S. action was rationalized on the basis

that other programs (e.g., the B-1 bomber) would restore the balance or that Soviet superiority in ICBMs would not have strategic importance. Some analysts continue to hope that the SALT III negotiations will constrain the Soviets in the post-1985 period. Still others believe that desperation strategies, such as "launch on warning," are all that is required to deter the Soviets.[13] The net effect of such views has been the opening of a significant gap in the balance of strategic power. *Figure 3* presents a model of the real world of U.S. reaction time. Even if the U.S. were to begin now to modernize its ICBM force, the balance would not be restored before 1990 unless the Soviets were to reduce the level of their power. Barring such a development, every year of additional waiting means that the relative balance will decline further and the time when the balance can be restored will be further delayed. It appears that the United States is now pinning its hopes on SALT III and the negotiation process as the principal way to restore the strategic balance.[14]

An alternative strategy which the U.S. could have followed in the past and which it must follow in the future is to have a range of available options which reduce the time for fielding new systems. One element of this strategy lies in an aggressive R&D program consisting of subsystem development and tests of weapon system prototypes. Another lies in the availability of "quick fixes." The lead time for programs which in essence constitute modernization of components or subsystems can be considerably shorter than for fielding new systems. Software programs, for example, can lead to improvements in missile guidance accuracy with a lead time as short as one to two years. Given several alternative programs (i.e., modernization or the fielding of a new system), a decision to react to a Soviet advance can be made shortly after assessing the physical evidence from Soviet tests. The budget and procurement cycle can then be accelerated to field a

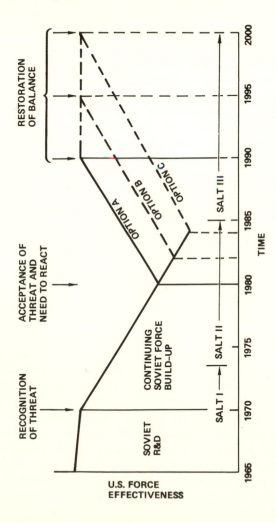

Figure 3. Actual Model

new system in a short time (see Alternative B, *Figure 2*) and thus prevent the Soviets from upsetting the strategic balance.[15]

It is obviously the case that over a period of several decades there will be continuing opposition to research and development programs which do not have as their clearly defined goal the deployment of new operating forces. The United States, however, will need programs with the goal of deterring research and development efforts in the U.S.S.R. It must be made clear to the Soviets that they will gain no advantage by advancing from the R&D phase to the deployment phase of any specific system. This technological strategy requires acceptance of the basic approach that the role of R&D is to give the U.S. time to respond without panic and the resulting high cost solutions if Soviet programs threaten basic American objectives. Employment of a balanced R&D program would enable the U.S. to respond without deploying more power in its operating forces.

As seen from the vantage point of a long-term R&D program, the range of efforts over an extended period would include concept definition, technical feasibility studies, and examination of key aspects such as reliability, but would stop short of actual deployment. There would thus be several programs at various stages of maturity—over, say, a decade—which would gradually replace existing R&D programs with new efforts without ever going the full route of systems acquisition and fielding. *Figure 4* presents an illustration of this time relationship. Such a time-phased, integrated effort would provide the U.S. with a capability to respond to the unexpected in an orderly way, and at the same time would provide the option of not spending large sums of money for full deployment unless such deployment were absolutely required.

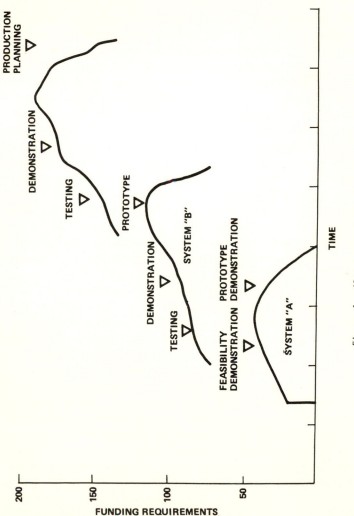

Figure 4. Alternative R&D Programs

COST IMPLICATIONS

It has been well known for many years that the conceptual phase of a new weapon system is the least expensive part of the process of system acquisition. Production and deployment have been the most expensive phases of the process in the past. On the other hand, research and development, up to the point of deployment, can also require sizable expenditures of funds. In an arms control environment, a new perspective on this problem will in fact be required in future decades because the number of strategic forces deployed will be reduced, thus altering the comparison of the research and development effort and the system acquisition effort. R&D will no longer be just an introductory phase of a program, but should have several goals of its own—i.e., to provide options to be used only if a response to Soviet actions is needed, and to act as a deterrent to Soviet R&D programs. Keeping options open, however, could well require R&D funding equal to the amount needed for actual deployment. To view this approach to the lead time problem in another way, R&D funds could be invested in different modes for ensuring force survivability so that the level of deployed power could be kept low while still remaining adequate. Thus, for a given level of funding, several programs could be pursued simultaneously without impacting on the strategic balance, unless such an impact were required. This approach is illustrated in *Figures* 5 and 6.

Strategic offensive forces which have different basing modes for survival are the subject of *Figures* 5 and 6. The U.S. presently maintains a triad of three strategic forces, based in submarines, on airfields, and in silos. If the U.S. were to have only two strategic forces, it would have to deploy more weapons in each of them in order to have enough weapons remaining in the case of a Soviet "break—out" or achievement of technological surprise which would negate one of the forces. With

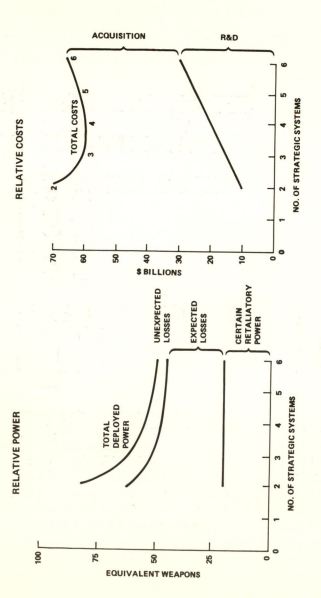

Figure 5. Comparison of Deployed Power and Costs for Various Numbers of Strategic Systems

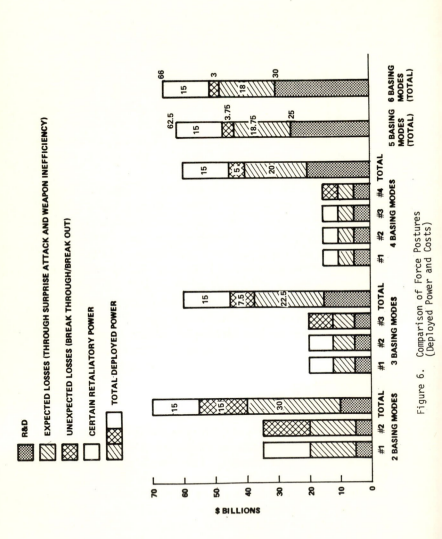

Figure 6. Comparison of Force Postures
(Deployed Power and Costs)

three force legs, the U.S. deploys less power and will still have sufficient power remaining if one force is threatened by a breakthrough. With four forces, the total deployed power could be even lower since, again, the U.S. would not be dependent on any one leg.

It is true that the combined investment in R&D is higher when there are more force types. The R&D cost for four forces is higher than for two; but, on the other hand, the total investment in R&D and deployment is less. Additionally, the number of deployed weapons is less for four force types than for two, as shown in *Figure 5*.

Figures 5 and *6* reveal a number of points. As the number of basing modes increases, the aggregate number of surviving weapons also increases. It is always necessary to deploy more forces than the number required for assured retaliatory power, but the size of this hedge decreases as the number of basing modes increases, thus making possible a reduction in total deployed power. A vigorous R&D program for multiple basing modes can reduce the hedge against "unexpected" losses, once again resulting in less deployed power. There would appear to be an optimum strategic force which has in each basing mode an equal amount of power, measured in terms of the number of targets which can be destroyed. However, the reduction in deployed power made possible by increasing the number of basing modes requires higher R&D costs; thus, as the number increases to five or six basing modes the total cost is higher than for three or four modes. The implications of these factors for the SALT process are two—fold: the U.S. should press for reductions in numbers so as to reduce the level of expected losses in the event of attack, and should keep its R&D options open for the development of additional modes of survival for the forces needed for retaliation.

Those analysts who propose that the U.S. have only one basing mode for its strategic forces (missile-carrying nuclear submarines are favored by some) should recognize that they are in effect proposing an unlimited budget for strategic systems. Even a reduction to two forces would be more costly than the present triad. On the other hand, those who favor a reduction in the number of deployed weapons are implicitly requiring higher R&D spending on strategic weapons; and if five or six basing modes are required to counter Soviet advances, higher total costs will result. These principles apply to Soviet force planning also, and because they have many basing modes for their offensive weapons the Soviets do spend more on strategic forces. The Soviets also have damage limiting forces—i.e., forces which reduce the amount of damage the U.S. could inflict in retaliation—which include active defenses (air defense, ASW, ABM, and an anti-satellite system [ASAT]); passive defenses (civil defense and dispersal); and offensive weapons (ICBMs, SLBMs, bombers, and Cruise missiles). The Soviets thus have a flexible force completely hedged and dynamic to incorporate new technology.

In summary, it is useful to recount the principles of the technological strategy which the U.S. should pursue in the future. The United States should have a broad base of technology which—if its utilization is properly timed and phased—can lead to force survival. Additionally, the deployment of U.S. forces in three or four survivable basing modes will result in lower total costs than will deployment in a lower or higher number of modes, but R&D costs will be higher than for programs which have as their objective acquisition and deployment of more weapons. Finally, deployed raw power can be reduced without degrading the performance of the total strategic system if it must someday be used.

An additional factor must be considered. At lower levels of force deployment, the individual weapon systems must be at the highest possible level of readiness, reliability, and effectiveness. These goals are best attained through a vigorous R&D program, especially one which has a high standard of testing of components and systems.

RANGE OF SYSTEMS

The dynamics of any arms control environment which provides the context for the construction of an American R&D program are extremely important. It is crucial that all weapons which have an impact on the balance of forces, and not just those which are "negotiable," be included in arms control negotiations. It must be recognized that not all existing offensive weapon systems which are "strategic," in the sense that they can attack the homeland of the opposing super-power, are now covered by the current on-going arms control process. Additionally, it is important to include those present weapons, as well as those new and emerging systems, which in the past would have been classified as "tactical" but which are in fact "strategic." A new term—"gray area" systems—has been invented for these weapons.[16] As more attention is given to this problem, it will be seen that many Soviet weapons are and have been in this "gray area."

Only the U.S. triad of SLBMs, ICBMs, and bombers (including those with Cruise missiles), and part of the Soviet forces of ICBMs, submarines, and bombers, are included in the SALT negotiations. The Soviets, how-ever, have hundreds of additional launchers not covered by SALT which can be used to attack the Continental U.S.[17] Among these launchers are Backfire bombers (some carrying air-launched Cruise missiles), submarine-launched Cruise missiles, surface-launched Cruise mis-siles, submarine-launched ballistic missiles in older boats, some unknown number of SS-16 mobile ICBMs, and some unknown number of Fractional Orbit Bom-bardment Systems (FOBS). Additionally, some Soviet ALCMs are carried by long-range bombers but, because they are of shorter range than those which the U.S. is developing (i.e., less than 600 kilometers), they are not included in the Soviet MIRV totals utilized in SALT. These weapons can all be used against American cities and military installations, even though some probably cannot be effective against American ICBMs in silos.[18]

The air defenses on both sides are also not included in SALT. The U.S. effectively dismantled its defenses against bombers and Cruise missiles beginning in the 1960s, when it eliminated its surface-to-air missiles and their command systems, failed to modernize its fighter interceptor force, and downgraded its command and control system for air defenses. In contrast, the Soviets continue to modernize their defenses. The arms control process obviously does not include passive defensive measures such as civil defense and the dispersal of industry.[19]

In summary, the range of systems which should be considered is far broader than that encompassed by the current SALT process. It is therefore necessary to look at the total Soviet strategic force structure and the on-going Soviet R&D programs in order to understand the potential threats which the U.S. might face. At the onset it is important to point out that the United States need not respond on a system-by-system basis or even on a technology-by-technology basis. In structuring a technological strategy for the U.S. in an arms control environment, attention must be focused on those critical developments which could lead to rapid force deployment or force employment which would disturb or destroy the strategic balance. In order to understand which of these issues is the most important, it is necessary to examine the options available to the Soviets.

The Soviet military force program covers nearly all conceivable weapon systems developments and acquisitions, and their R&D program includes nearly all known areas of interest, from basic science to applications.[20]

Furthermore, the Soviets adhere to the technological strategy of continually modernizing each element of their forces, so that their total development program includes a range of new concepts, a number of technological developments, and the programmed modernization of forces or the replacement of specific weapons by entirely new weapons. This strategy operates in all areas, from hand guns to ballistic missiles to satellite systems. In the realm of technology, the Soviets are investigating everything from computers and software to the most recent advances in nuclear physics. Some of these latter advances may be as important as the breakthroughs in the understanding of physics which occurred in the 1930s and which led to the nuclear fission process. It is useful to look at some of these Soviet options a little more closely.

Strategic Defensive Forces

Soviet defensive programs include both active and passive defenses. Among the active defenses are anti-aircraft systems, anti-ballistic missile systems, anti-satellite programs with their supporting ground control network, and the necessary satellites for the command, control, and operation of each of these aspects of active defense. These forces are now being modernized, and the Soviets have continued their research and development on anti-ballistic missile systems. The 1972 SALT I Treaty on Limitations of Anti-Ballistic Missile Systems and the subsequent 1974 ABM agreement restricted the Soviets to the current deployment of a maximum of 100 launchers at one site, but it did not constrain R&D. Soviet moderization programs include experimentation with new components to upgrade their current ABM and such new approaches as the utilization of lasers as ABM systems.

The net effect of this on-going and far-reaching R&D program is that the U.S. must be prepared to guard against a break-out of capability which would make the

Soviet ABM much more effective than the present limited deployment. Such a break-out could occur either via modernization of the present system and deployment of large numbers, or by pursuit of an entirely new approach, such as an application of laser technology to ABM. These developments would make it difficult for U.S. retaliatory strikes to penetrate Soviet defenses. If the United States were to operate at reduced levels of forces, the Soviet defenses might cause U.S. deployment of more penetration aids or more re-entry vehicles, so as to insure American ability to mount a successful attack on designated targets after penetrating the Soviet ABM.

The Soviets also have an extensive program for active air defenses, which are not constrained by treaty. The Soviets have deployed some ten thousand surface-to-air missiles and thousands of interceptor aircraft, all of which are controlled by an extensive ground control network and command and control system.[21] Given the potential that the U.S. may deploy Cruise missiles as part of its strategic offensive forces, it is believed that the Soviets are presently upgrading their active air defenses to negate Cruise missiles.[22] Once again, the Soviets have several options for achieving this purpose: expanded deployment of the current systems; redeployment—for strategic air defense of the Soviet homeland—of some of the air defense systems presently accompanying the Soviet ground forces in the occupied countries; or engagement in an active program to develop new weapons which could be employed either for the defense of the U.S.S.R. or as part of the Soviet offensive striking power for an attack on NATO or the People's Republic of China. Additionally, it should be anticipated that the Soviets will attempt to apply new developments in technology—perhaps, again, lasers or beam weapons—to modernize their future air defenses.

With respect to anti-satellite systems (ASAT), the Soviets have an on-going program which has been tested many times and which has demonstrated the capability of attacking satellites in a variety of orbits and at different altitudes. While this system presently appears to be capable only against satellites at low altitudes, there is always the potential that some other system, such as an anti-ballistic missile system, could be modified to create a weapon with more reach which could attack satellites at higher altitudes than can the present Soviet system. The strategic impact of the present system and current and future modernization efforts pose a continuing threat to American satellite systems, upon which the U.S. may depend during periods of crisis or in order to mount retaliatory strikes in the event of a Soviet attack.

In the area of passive defensive measures, attention has recently been called to the revitalized Soviet program for civil defense. The U.S. agreed to the SALT I Treaty and the Interim Agreement on the Limitation of Strategic Offensive Arms on the basis of a concept called "mutual assured destruction." This concept assumes that the population of each superpower is held in hostage by the offensive weapons of the other; the fear of the loss of large numbers of its own people thus deters each government from attacking the other country. The Soviet civil defense program undercuts this concept. Paul H. Nitze has stated, in fact, that the Soviets estimate that their civil defense program should hold their casualties in the event of a nuclear exchange to 3 or 4 percent of their population.[23] If the Soviets are correct, this civil defense capability is in effect the equivalent of an ABM system in that it negates the effectiveness of U.S. strategic offensive weapons. Soviet passive defense includes the hardening of headquarters for the command and control of nearly all elements of the Soviet strategic forces, including the Strategic Rocket Forces and the Air Defense Forces, and the headquarters for Armies up to the Politburo.[24] Another facet of the program is the hardening of selected industries and the dispersal of industry so that the Soviet industrial base is less vulnerable to U.S. retaliation than American industry is to Soviet attack. Modernization programs will further nearly all these measures in the future.[25]

The Soviet space program is much more active than the American program. In past years, the Soviets have launched four times as many satellites per year as has the U.S. Some analysts believe that this increased rate is required because the Soviet satellites are less effective and have shorter lives than U.S. satellites. That opinion is hard to substantiate, however, because the status of the health of each of the Soviet satellites is not known. As one effect of a vigorous, continuous program, the Soviets have large numbers of satellites in orbit for each specific function. This proliferation would provide increased survivability in the event the U.S. were to attempt to engage in ASAT operations (a contingency which lies a decade in the future). The range of functions covered includes surveillance, weather, communications, navigation, and geodesy. More than a decade ago, the Soviets developed bombs-in-orbit (FOBS). The Soviets recently established a new record of total number of hours accumulated in space by their Cosmonauts. Additionally, as has already been mentioned, the Soviet space program includes an active ASAT. To provide a counter-balance to these Soviet system and research and development programs, the main U.S. concern lies in protecting its satellites against Soviet anti-satellite operations, either the present interceptor or an eventual laser system which could be either ground-based or space-based.[26]

Strategic Offensive Forces

Soviet forces are deployed in a wide variety of basing modes and are dispersed at many points around the globe. As in the case of other force elements already discussed, the Soviets are continually modernizing existing weapons and are conducting active programs to replace them with newer systems. With respect to ICBMs, Moscow has in existence a full range of four new weapons and has started testing a fifth generation of ICBMs. A new submarine and submarine-launched ballistic missile were recently unveiled. The manned bomber force is being modernized through the deployment of the Backfire, and there have been reports that the Soviets have been adapting their supersonic transport technology to development of a supersonic bomber. One version of the new generation of ICBMs has been deployed in a mobile mode; it is thus not confined to the fixed silos which were agreed upon in the SALT I Agreement of 1972 and the subsequent Vladivostok Accord. Given the past history of Soviet weapon development and the limited American understanding of current Soviet R&D, it should be anticipated that each of these elements will in the future be modernized and eventually replaced. By the end of the century Soviet forces will look entirely different, with a whole new range of weapon systems in the field.

Theater Forces

Since the early days of World War II, the U.S. has drawn a distinction between "strategic" and "tactical" forces. The term "theater" forces is now gaining acceptance in place of "tactical." It should be recognized, however, that any use of armed forces by one of the superpowers can be strategic. This is especially true if forces are employed in Europe or the Middle East, with attendant risks of bringing the "strategic" forces of both superpowers into the conflict. As has already been mentioned, the distinction between types of forces has become blurred by "gray area" systems which can be used either in conflicts in Europe or in attacks on the homelands of the superpowers. It is important to point out that in Europe the Soviets have an overwhelming numerical superiority in systems which can deliver nuclear weapons. The Eurostrategic balance is approximately as follows:[27]

	USSR	NATO
Intermediate Range Ballistic Missiles	600[1]	146[2]
Medium-Range Bombers	600	60
Land-Based Aircraft	1000	400[3]
Naval Aircraft	400	200[4]
Cruise Missiles	300	0

1. SS-4/5s are being replaced with MIRVed SS-20s, with a total force projected to reach 1000 boosters and 3000 weapons.
2. 64 French SLBMs, 18 French Medium Range Ballistic Missiles, and 64 British SLBMs.
3. Only a few of these aircraft can reach targets in the Soviet Union.
4. Assumes 5 U.S. aircraft carriers deployed to Europe..

The number of NATO military installations which the Soviets might target with nuclear weapons is, at most, approximately three hundred. The Soviets presently have ten delivery systems for each target, and when the SS-20 has been fully fielded they will have ten weapons for each target in this system alone. The elements of Soviet offensive forces are also being modernized. The Soviet motivation for such tremendous capability, enabling them to destroy every military installation in NATO ten times over, continues to be a mystery in the West.

Moreover, these offensive forces must be considered in conjunction with the active and passive Soviet defenses discussed above. The Soviet defenses can be employed to defend the U.S.S.R. against NATO forces deployed in Europe just as they can be against U.S. strategic forces based in the Continental United States.

Implications

The combination of a) the disparity in lead time[28] which permits the Soviets to field new forces more quickly than the United States, and b) the wide range of options which the Soviets are covering both in deployment and in research and development, makes it imperative that the U.S. have a balanced R&D program. U.S. goals should include both the continuing survivability of American offensive power and the weapons performance adequate for the achievement of desired effects if the U.S. fails to deter and it becomes necessary to engage in active military operations. This is especially true if one of the American objectives in arms negotiations—a large reduction in the number of weapons employed on both sides—is reached.

B. VERIFICATION

The Strategic Arms Limitation process, including the SALT I Treaty and Interim Agreement and the Vladivostok Agreement, has instituted a new type of safeguard, in that each superpower has agreed that it will not interfere with the other's national technical means of verifying that the other side is adhering to the provisions of the treaties and agreements. The entire subject of verification is a complex one, and the purpose goes beyond simply determining whether or not a treaty has been violated. What is crucial is to determine whether such violations have disturbed the strategic balance and have led to an unexpected advantage on the part of the violator. Small violations on minor subjects are important only insofar as they indicate intent to violate the major provisions of the treaty or are an indication of some cover and deception scheme to conceal that a major violation has been made. Consequently, the term "adequate verification" is normally used in reference to the situation in which the national technical means can detect in time a violation of the treaty which could cause a fundamental change in the strategic balance.[29] One of the key problems which will undoubtedly arise with respect to U.S ratification of the

SALT II Treaty will be questions about the possibility of insuring adequate verification.

While it is certainly important to know whether a treaty has been violated, it is perhaps even more important to know that adequate measures exist to provide safeguards against such violations, especially if they are major in nature. The process of "breaking out" of treaty bounds can come through the deployment of more weapons than are permitted under the treaty or agreement. Soviet deployment of a large number of land-based ICBMs in violation of the numerical ceilings on total launchers or on MIRVed launchers could well pose additional threats to U.S. strategic forces. Similarly, an increase in the number of anti-ballistic missile launchers or perhaps even deployment of these launchers in new locations could provide a major change in the strategic balance.

GRAY AREA SYSTEMS

Gray area systems—i.e., weapon systems which are defined as "tactical" or "theater" weapons but whose performance characteristics in fact enable them to be employed as "strategic" systems—present additional verification problems. The Soviet SS-20 serves as an important example. This missile is in actuality a version of the SS-16 ICBM; it has been reported, in fact, that the physical differences between the two ballistic missiles are almost minor from an external point of view. Consequently, it would be possible for the Soviets to greatly increase their strategic forces by deploying more SS-16s under the guise of being SS-20s. (The present SALT process does not include the SS-20 since it is classified as a mid-range ballistic missile.) There is thus concern that such ambiguity could lead to a major violation of treaty provisions. As has already been noted, such a violation could be especially significant during a future period in which the U.S. had greatly reduced the numbers of weapons in its strategic arsenal.

The Backfire is also an ambiguous weapon system. The Soviets assert that the Backfire is a medium-range bomber designed for theater operations, and thus insist that it not be included in the SALT II numerical limitations. U.S. analysis of the Backfire's performance, as deduced from its technical capabilities, leads nevertheless to the conclusion that the bomber has a range which far exceeds that of a normal medium bomber and that it could fly as far as 6,000 miles. According to this assessment, it would have the ability to attack targets in the U.S. and to land at bases in Latin America. Additionally, the Backfire could be refueled in flight and thus engage in two-way missions, with return to the U.S.S.R.[30] Despite these factors, the U.S. has assumed in the SALT II negotiations that the Soviet heavy bomber force is relatively small, on the order of 140 bombers. The Backfire—with a production rate of some 50 per year and an eventual force of over 400 bombers possible during the period of the SALT II Treaty—could, however, pose a significant threat to the U.S., particularly in a period of reduction of the types of weapons presently included in the SALT process. It has been reported that Brezhnev has asserted that the Soviets will give the United States written assurance that the Backfire will not be used to threaten the U.S. There is, however, no way to verify whether or not the Soviets will actually abide by such a statement.

The whole question of verification has thus been clouded by these gray area systems, and it will be necessary to exercise special care to provide adequate safeguards against these implicit dangers to the strategic balance in future decades.

C. R&D OPTIONS

The problem of research and development in an arms control environment is paradoxical. Restrictions on R&D for future weaponry could result in a reduction in the number and effectiveness of deployed systems; and without research and development the United States might be surprised by some advance in technology which could disturb the strategic balance. Consequently, there are strong incentives for a vigorous R&D program. Opponents of research and development assert, on the other hand, that once R&D is accepted as an essential part of the SALT environment, one side can achieve a break-out into a new strategic posture which disturbs the balance; therefore, according to this view, R&D should be limited.

It should be clearly recognized that—because the onrush of technology will continue to generate advances which can be applied to strategic forces—limiting R&D is not in fact realistic. Although the U.S. SLBM force, for example, is at present almost completely survivable because the submarines are difficult to locate, continued improvements in Soviet ASW technology could permit the Soviets to determine the location of and threaten these submarines. To understand whether or not that threat is developing, and to achieve new measures for survivability, the U.S. must pursue its own ASW technology. There is thus a need for a strong mobilization base of adequate research and development, both to understand the nature of advances in the state of the art and to ensure options which can be applied to counter some unanticipated development by the other side.

DEFENSIVE OPTIONS

The United States now has a vigorous R&D program

which includes a sizable effort devoted to understanding the nature of anti-ballistic missile technology and an investigation of concepts for new defensive systems. The U.S. does not, however, have the counterpart air defense technology.

It is true that the U.S. does have on-going weapon systems for theater air defense—i.e., surface-to-air missiles and new interceptor aircraft. These systems are not being applied, however, to the defense of the Continental United States. Another basic asymmetry lies in the fact that the U.S. cannot rapidly move the air defenses which are being constructed for the European theater back to the Continental U.S. to provide augmentation of an integrated air defense net, since the present theater air defenses are sized for the NATO problem and there is no excess that could be redeployed for defense of the U.S. Until now the United States has assumed that—because the Soviet bomber force has been small in number and of lower capability than the massive Soviet ICBM force—defense against Soviet attacking bombers was of secondary importance. If the U.S. is serious about reductions in the SALT III period, however, the importance of an adequate defensive posture must be reconsidered. Given the ambiguous potential employment of the Backfire bomber, maintenance of a strategic balance in the area of defenses could be critical, especially if that weapon system is not included in the SALT II and SALT III ceilings.

A potential way of leap-frogging this problem is to consider advances in new types of weapons—principally lasers and beam weapons—as means for providing active air defenses against future Soviet weapons. The U.S. has been pursuing the laser weapon technology for more than a decade and has devices in the stage of demonstration and application, but still has not made the essential advances necessary to apply this technology to a deployed weapon system. Beam weapon technology in the U.S. falls in a second generation which may be available around the end of the century.

To consider another aspect of the defense problem, the Soviets presently have a significant lead over the U.S. in their ability to destroy satellite systems. The U.S. does not have a counterpart capability, but it does have a research and development program underway to develop and acquire such a system, if it is needed.

The potential that lasers may be adapted to weapons for the negation of satellites creates a concern for the future. This is especially true if lasers of adequate size and power can be deployed in space. Space provides a less demanding environment for the operation of chemical laser weapons, since the absence of an atmosphere makes it possible to attain destructive effects at longer ranges. Given the growing dependence of American military forces on satellites for a variety of functions, it is crucial that the U.S. have the potential of acquiring such space-based laser weapons and of developing essential countermeasures. The future potential of space warfare is thus a real one, and should provide incentives for the U.S. to conduct a comprehensive R&D effort in this area.

Finally, in the category of defensive measures, anti-submarine warfare to defend against Soviet SLBMs continues to be an all-important question. Technology for surveillance of the oceans will be essential for the future in any arms control environment. The Soviets have developed an ocean surveillance satellite which may have applications to ASW operations. The U.S. must make efforts to understand the potential of ocean surveillance technology, and must be prepared to institute the countermeasures which may be necessary for the continuation of the highest possible degree of invulnerability of American SLBMs.

OFFENSIVE SYSTEMS

The U.S. presently has programs for the modernization of two elements of its strategic forces. With the demise of the B-1, the Cruise missile is being developed to provide the manned bomber force with stand-off weapons of extreme accuracy which can, if required, attack targets in the U.S.S.R., including even hardened silos. The submarine force is being modernized by the acquisition of both the Trident submarine and a Trident missile.

The modernization of the land-based ICBM force is a major remaining area. Here the MX program provides the key to the future U.S. strategic posture, for this program, if properly developed and deployed, can provide the ideal way to attain two of the basic American goals in arms control: strategic stability and arms reduction.

The SALT II Treaty currently under negotiation will probably terminate in 1985, while the MX system, short of herculean effort to acquire it, probably cannot be effectively deployed until post-1986. Thus, the MX will be a SALT III program.[31] Some of the MX design features have been greatly influenced by U.S. arms control objectives and by the constraints agreed to in prior negotiations and agreements (SALT I and Vladivostok) and during the SALT II process. The U.S. in pursuing the MX program is developing the means not only for the continued deterrence of strategic nuclear war but also for reductions in the amount of deployed strategic power. In combining these characteristics, the MX is unique and the first program of its kind.

A principal objective of the MX program is a new mode of ICBM basing which can assure—in the face of a continued buildup of Soviet strategic offensive power—the survivability of an adequate number of weapons. "Crisis stability" is an important consideration. There is concern that a deep crisis might lead the Soviets to conclude that to attack would be more advantageous than to restrain their actions. If U.S. ICBMs are very likely to survive an onslaught, the rationality of a Soviet decision not to attack will be increased. Survival is thus the key to stability in general and to crisis stability in particular. It is imperative that the U.S. apply its technology to ensure the highest possible confidence in the survivability of American ICBMs.

The technological strategy being pursued in the MX program complements the concurrent U.S. attempt to limit through treaties and agreements important aspects of Soviet strategic power. The U.S. is using its technology to develop a system which will in one sense make the Soviet silo-based ICBM force obsolete, in that the Soviets will be unable to view their force as a powerful coercive tool in crises and conflict situations. U.S. technology can thus prevent the Soviet use of ICBMs to attain strategic dominance. The Soviets might conclude that their best technological strategy is the deployment of a more survivable ICBM force, perhaps of a different design than the United States has chosen but with the same objective of maintaining survival. When both sides have their ICBMs in highly survivable basing modes, stability at the political, at the crisis, and at the deterrence levels will be enhanced and there will be incentives for reducing the number of weapons on both sides. As has been stated above, this technological strategy as embodied in the MX program is the best way to attain the goals of continued deterrence and reduction of levels of strategic forces.

Stability will be enforced by the deployment of the MX missile in MPS—i.e., the construction of a large number of aimpoints which the Soviets must attack in any attempt to eliminate the American land-based force. The present Titan and Minuteman silo force is restricted under SALT I to 1,054 launch points. The location of these points and their characteristics in terms of hardness are well known to Soviet planners. Additionally, in-depth studies of Soviet attack tactics against American silos indicate that in coming years the Soviets could, with the use of as few as 2,000 weapons, reduce the effectiveness of the U.S. silo force to very low levels. Other studies have postulated that the Soviets could attack with three weapons on each silo and thus effectively eliminate the U.S. silo force; even after having conducted such a heavy attack, according to these studies, the Soviets would retain a reserve of thousands of ICBM re-entry vehicles in their hardened silos.

Once American ICBMs are deployed in an MPS mode—what has been called a "shell game"—it will no longer be possible for an attacker to destroy a large number of U.S. silos by launching only a small number of MIRVed missiles. The attacker would instead have to use his entire MIRVed ICBM arsenal to attack a few missiles. The MPS approach to survivability thus puts the "MIRV genie back in the bottle."

Successful deterrence in the future arms control environment will also require that the United States have an adequate Command, Control, and Communications system. At the core of a sufficient C^3 posture are the abilities to understand the nature of conflict, to make the correct decisions so as to cope with various military situations, to effectively command forces to operate, and to know and evaluate the outcome of such operations so that subsequent efforts can also be effective and appropriate. Over the years the U.S. has developed and deployed a panoply of sensors (ground-based, space-based, and airborne) for warning of attack and for provision of the data needed for decision making during the unfolding of conflict. In addition, the U.S. has a communications network with redundant paths, including satellite systems, for collecting data and for transmitting orders. This network has been expanded as the Soviet threat has grown. In years to come the U.S. will need to continue to modernize the sensor systems, the communications network, and the control facilities.

As long as the Soviets have an anti-satellite system, the U.S. must be concerned about the vulnerability of its satellites and the connecting links which transmit satellite data to decision makers. Redundant paths and mobile receiving stations may be needed. This element of U.S. forces could become even more critical in the future if the U.S. is successful in reducing forces, for there will then be a premium placed on operating at a low level of forces with high reliability and effectiveness.

Finally, it should be recognized that even the modernization of U.S. strategic power, as discussed above, is far from the end of the process. The two basic factors in the geopolitical situation—Soviet enmity and the onrush of technology—promise to be of long duration. As R&D programs are implemented the U.S. must seek additional technological avenues to strengthen and ensure U.S. security. Arms control measures, treaties, and limitations will create an even greater need for a sound, dynamic, long-range American technological strategy.

D. CONCLUSIONS

Many of the major issues in SALT II have been negotiated, but difficult problems still lie ahead. Conflicting views on Cruise missiles and the Backfire bomber must be resolved. Fears that the provisions of the Protocol will be extended automatically beyond the end of SALT II must be overcome. Several proposals have been discussed by members of Congress; the main point is that the U.S. should retain the option of deploying mobile ICBMs after the expiration of the Protocol period. It is highly probable that these issues will be resolved and that a Treaty will be submitted to the Congress for ratification in 1979.

If a SALT II Treaty is submitted, it can be expected that Congress will take actions similar to that undertaken in the ratification of SALT I. It will, in other words, define guidelines for SALT III and will approve a program of system development and acquisition to provide safeguards against the deficiencies of the proposed SALT II Treaty.

The SALT III guidelines should include at least the following points:

1) The range of strategic offensive systems to be limited should be expanded to include all Soviet forces which can attack the United States.
2) Defensive forces should be included, both air defenses and ASW. (The ABM Treaty is of unlimited duration and ABM need not be included here. ASATs are the subject of a separate negotiation process.)
3) Passive defense measures (principally, civil defense) should be included.
4) Limits on forces should be set at a very low level (e.g., 1,000 strategic offensive weapons).

Additionally, the United States Defense Program should be funded to include:

1) Full-scale development of the MX missile.
2) Development of a new basing mode for the MX missile, in the form of the Multiple Protective Structures.
3) Development of a new program for nuclear powered submarines carrying ballistic missiles (SSBNs).
4) Initiation of a new program for a manned penetrating bomber.
5) Inclusion in the technology base of a vigorous ABM and ASAT R&D program.
6) Continued high priority for laser and "energy beam" technologies.
7) A C^3 program which should provide the base for

improved surveillance, including warning and attack assessment, and survivable communications.
8) Emphasis on research for new technical break-throughs.

The SALT negotiation process should therefore lead to limits on forces, and a "Safeguards Program" should create the base for dynamic stability. *Together, these efforts can lead to the achievement of the two basic U.S. objectives—continued security, but at reduced levels of weapons.*

NOTES

1 The Department of Defense proposed and the Congress approved a number of "SALT Related Adjustments to Strategic Programs" for Fiscal Years 1972 and 1973. Included were cancellation of three programs for construction of the Safeguard Ballistic Missile Defense Program at Malmstrom and Grand Forks, and increases in six other programs. See "Military Implications of the Treaty on Limitations of Anti-Ballistic Missile Systems and the Interim Agreement on Limitations on Strategic Offensive Arms," Hearings before the Committee on Armed Services, U.S. Senate, 92nd Congress, 2nd Session (Washington: U.S. Government Printing Office, 1972), p. 17. (The $543 million made available from cancellation of the Safeguard ABM Program was spent on the other strategic programs.)

2 Over the years the U.S. has used a variety of measures of balance (mutual assured destruction, essential equivalence, etc.). Perceptions of relative status is an inherent element of balance. Paul H. Nitze discusses the problem of "balance" in "The Global Military Balance," *Proceedings of the Academy of Political Science*, Vol. 33 (March 1978), pp. 4-14.

3 As Lewis Richardson has pointed out, a nation would build arms guided by ambition, grievances, and hostilities even if another nation posed no threat to it. Cited in Thomas L. Saaty, *Mathematical Models of Arms Control and Disarmament* (New York: Wiley and Sons, 1968), p. 46.

4 In *Arms Control and Technological Change: Elements of a New Approach*, Adelphi Paper No. 146 (London: International Institute for Strategic Studies, Summer 1978), p.30, Christoph Bertram states that "It [East-West arms control] is incapable of coping with the qualitative arms competition."

5 One of the major technological developments since World War II is the invention and application of the LASER (Light

Amplification by Stimulated Emission of Radiation), which uses matter at the atomic or molecular level to generate coherent electromagnetic radiation in the ultra-violet, violet, and infrared regions of the spectrum. Lasers have been developed to guide weapons to targets; the use of lasers to destroy targets such as missiles or aircraft is now being investigated. "Beam" weapons would employ subatomic particles which would be accelerated to very high energy levels. The particles would be beamed at the target at or near the speed of light. See Milton Copulos, "Laser and Charged Particle Beam Weapons," *Journal of Social and Political Studies*, Vol. 2, Number 4 (Winter 1977), pp. 311-319; *Science*, October 8, 1976, p. 166, and April 22, 1977, pp. 407-408; and the six part series on beam weapons published in *Aviation Week and Space Technology*, October 2, October 9, October 16, October 23, October 30, and November 6, 1978.

6 In his January 1978 study, Congressman Les Aspin shows in detail the present asymmetry in the strategic positions of the U.S. and the Soviet Union. While the U.S. has no on-going programs to protect against the failure of SALT, the Soviets have several. Aspin concludes that the U.S. must achieve a SALT II accord, for it will be worse off without an agreement. That conclusion does not, however, apply to the Soviets. In other words, Dimitri Simes is correct when he observes, "Bargaining skills mean little in the absence of bargaining chips." (*Foreign Policy*, Fall 1978, p.52.)

7 See U.S. Congress, Senate, Statement of John S. Foster, Director of Research and Engineering, Department of Defense, before the Subcommittee on Arms Control, International Law and Organization of the Committee on Foreign Relations, *Hearings on Arms Control Implications of Current U.S. Defense Budget*, 92nd Congress, 1st Session, June 16, June 17, July 13, and July 14, 1971, p. 49.

8 In the 1960s this author played a leading role in advocating the use of satellites for navigation. The concept was then called NAVSAT (Navigation Satellite). The program is now called NAVSTAR or the Global Positioning System (GPS). The user of the system will receive signals from several (three to four) satellites, correlate the signals through a computer program, and "read" his or her position. The accuracy of location and velocity will vary with the sophistication of the receiving and computing equipment. For aircraft, dynamic position location can be known to ten meters. The system is passive and can be used by thousands of "navigators" simultaneously, including satellites and missiles. The goal of this author was to provide the service eventually to aircraft of all sizes and to all ships and boats, including those of weekend sailors.

9 This is the view attributed to former Secretary of Defense Robert McNamara.

10 This is the assumption upon which Kosta Tsipis based his analysis in "Physics and Calculus of Countercity and Counterforce Attacks," *Science*, February 7, 1975, pp. 393-397. For a rebuttal, see R.J. Rummel, "Will the Soviet Union Soon Have a First-Strike Capability?", *Orbis*, Fall 1976, pp. 579-594.

11 For an example of this view, see the report by M. Callaham, B.T. Field, E. Hadjimichael, and K.M. Tsipis, *The MX Missile: An Arms Control Impact Statement* (Cambridge: Massachusetts Institute of Technology, March 1978), pp.8-12.

12 In the late 1950s some persons involved in ICBM developments and knowledgable of guidance technology assumed that fixed land-based systems (submarines in port, airfields, and silos) would eventually become vulnerable to highly accurate weapons, especially ballistic missiles using inertial systems and Cruise missiles employing combinations of techniques, including satellites. The solutions proposed—aircraft on airborne alert and mobile ICBMs—were based on mobility. An almost infinite set of concepts has since been examined, including rail-mobile and land-mobile basing, deployment in the Great Lakes, and sheltering deep in the Rockies. A number of concepts are still being studied, including air-mobile and land-mobile systems. The Multiple Protective Structure (MPS) concept is one option in the latter category, and involves movement of a few missiles among many silos.

13 See Al Hall, "The Case for an Improved ICBM," *Astronautics and Aeronautics*, February 1977, pp. 24-31, for a discussion of the rationale for this solution to U.S. vulnerability, as an adjunct to an ICBM system more survivable than the present Minuteman force.

14 One element of SALT II will be a Joint Statement of Principles and Guidelines for SALT III "to pursue further reductions in the ceilings and further qualitative limitations on strategic systems." See *The Strategic Arms Limitations Talks*, Department of State, Special Report No. 46, July 1978.

15 Those who believe that the U.S. is the engine of the so-called "action/reaction cycle" obviously will not agree with the foregoing analysis. The record shows, however, that the Soviets have made the most "firsts" since World War II in applying technology to strategic nuclear warfare: e.g., with the hydrogen bomb, the ballistic missile, ICBMs, the Fractional Orbit Bombardment System, satellites, ABM, the Anti-Satellite System, etc. If the United States were really in control of the strategic situation, it would not see its decisions driven by Soviet innovations but would gear its decisions to arms reductions.

16 For a discussion of this problem see the Atlantic Council Policy Paper, published in July 1978, entitled "Arms Control and Gray Area Weapon Systems." The case of some Soviet submarine-launched Cruise missiles illustrates this problem of ambiguity. These Cruise missiles are classified as "tactical"

because they were designed to "home" in on radars and thus destroy with nuclear weapons ships or land-based facilities. Such Cruise missiles can "home" on radars near New York, Washington, Boston, and San Francisco, and thus destroy the adjacent cities. Their use can therefore be "strategic." The "grayness" of these weapons comes not from their performance but from arbitrary U.S. classification as to how the Soviets can employ them.

17 For the details see *The Military Balance 1978-1979* (London: International Institute for Strategic Studies, 1978), pp. 8-10.

18 Failure to include these weapons gives the Soviets an additional advantage which follows from the strategic asymmetry of the geographies of the two countries: many U.S. urban industrial centers are located on the coasts, while those of the Soviet Union are deep in the interior.

19 President Carter announced in late 1978 a new program for U.S. civil defense. Critics of the decision asserted that he was trying to buy votes of "hawkish" Senators for SALT II.

20 John M. Collins and Anthony H. Cordesman, *Imbalance of Power* (San Rafael, Calif.: Presidio Press, 1978).

21 *The Military Balance 1978-1979*, p. 9.

22 The Soviets are attempting to use the SALT II process to constrain the range of U.S. Cruise missiles and thus to prevent the U.S. from making Soviet defenses less effective. For an analysis of Soviet aims in the SALT process, see William T. Lee, "Soviet Targeting Strategy and SALT," *Air Force*, September 1978, pp. 120ff.

23 Paul H. Nitze, "Deterring Our Deterrent," *Foreign Policy*, Winter 1976-1977, pp. 204-205.

24 *Soviet Civil Defense*, Department of State, Special Report No. 47, September 1978, p.2.

25 The issue of civil defense effectiveness has been much debated since Leon Gouré and William F. and Harriet Fast Scott pointed up U.S. neglect of the Soviet program. Recent analyses have been published by the Director of Central Intelligence, "Soviet Civil Defense," NI 78-10003, July 1978; and by the Department of State, as cited above. For a recent detailed study, see T.K. Jones and W. Scott Thompson, "Central War and Civil Defense," *Orbis*, Fall 1978, pp. 681-712.

26 Stockholm International Peace Research Institute (SIPRI), *Outer Space-Battlefield of the Future?* (New York: Crane, Russak & Co., 1978), pp. 167-179.

27 See Richard Burt, "The SS-20 and the Eurostrategic Balance," *The World Today*, February 1977; and Uwe Nerlich, *The Alliance and Europe: Part V, Nuclear Weapons and East-West Negotiations*, Adelphi Paper No. 120, Winter 1975-1976. Nerlich examines the issue of the so-called "Forward based systems" and the success of the Soviets to date in keeping their counterpart weapons out of the U.S.-Soviet negotiations. In 1972 a

spokesman for the Soviets objected to the concept of confining the Mutual and Balanced Force Reductions (MBFR)
negotiations to Central Europe. He correctly pointed out that
weapon systems outside that region (e.g., rocket forces) give
the problem a global scale. See Yu Kostko, "Mutual Force
Reductions in Europe," *Survival,* September/October 1972,
pp. 236-238.

28 Another way of characterizing the asymmetry is to point up
the disparity in program continuity. The Soviets have long had
an active, dynamic effort; the American effort, on the other
hand, is episodic in reaction to perceived Soviet developments.

29 See "SALT Negotiations," Hearings before the Committee on
Foreign Relations, U.S. Senate, Briefings by Cyrus R. Vance,
Secretary of State, and Ambassador Paul C. Warnke, Director,
Arms Control and Disarmament Agency, November 2 and 29,
1977; and *Verification: The Critical Element of Arms Control,*
U.S. Arms Control and Disarmament Agency, Publication No.
85, March 1976.

30 Les Aspin, "The Verification of the SALT II Agreement,"
Scientific American, February 1979, pp. 40-41.

31 It might be noted in passing that the debate on SALT II will
not recognize this time relationship; much confusion will result from the assumption that a system being pursued in the
research and development arena during SALT II will be deployed during the period of SALT II. The U.S. should use MX
for leverage on the Soviets in an attempt to achieve arms reductions in SALT III.

National Strategy Information Center, Inc.

PUBLICATIONS

Frank N. Trager, Editor
Dorothy E. Nicolosi, Associate Editor
Joyce E. Larson, Managing Editor

AGENDA PAPERS

Naval Race or Arms Control in the Indian Ocean? (Some Problems in Negotiating Naval Limitations) by Alvin J. Cottrell and Walter F. Hahn, September 1978

Power Projection: A Net Assessment of U.S. and Soviet Capabilities by W. Scott Thompson, April 1978

Understanding the Soviet Military Threat, How CIA Estimates Went Astray by William T. Lee, February 1977

Toward a New Defense for NATO, The Case for Tactical Nuclear Weapons, July 1976 (Out of print)

Seven Tracks to Peace in the Middle East by Frank R. Barnett, April 1975

Arms Treaties with Moscow: Unequal Terms Unevenly Applied? by Donald G. Brennan, April 1975 (Out of print)

Toward a U.S. Energy Policy by Klaus Knorr, March 1975 (Out of print)

133

Can We Avert Economic Warfare in Raw Materials? US Agriculture as a Blue Chip by William Schneider, July 1974

STRATEGY PAPERS

India: Emergent Power? by Stephen P. Cohen and Richard L. Park, June 1978

The Kremlin and Labor: A Study in National Security Policy by Roy Godson, November 1977

The Evolution of Soviet Security Strategy 1965-1975 by Avigdor Haselkorn, November 1977

The Geopolitics of the Nuclear Era by Colin S. Gray, September 1977

The Sino-Soviet Confrontation: Implications for the Future by Harold C. Hinton, September 1976

Food, Foreign Policy, and Raw Materials Cartels by William Schneider, February 1976

Strategic Weapons: An Introduction by Norman Polmar, October 1975 (Out of print)

Soviet Sources of Military Doctrine and Strategy by William F. Scott, July 1975

Detente: Promises and Pitfalls by Gerald L. Steibel, March 1975 (Out of print)

Oil, Politics and Sea Power: The Indian Ocean Vortex by Ian W.A.C. Adie, December 1974 (Out of print)

The Soviet Presence in Latin America by James D. Theberge, June 1974

The Horn of Africa by J. Bowyer Bell, Jr., December 1973

Research and Development and the Prospects for International Security by Frederick Seitz and Rodney W. Nichols, December 1973

Raw Material Supply in a Multipolar World by Yuan-li Wu, October 1973 (Out of print)

The People's Liberation Army: Communist China's Armed Forces by Angus M. Fraser, August 1973 (Out of print)

Nuclear Weapons and the Atlantic Alliance by Wynfred Joshua, May 1973

How to Think About Arms Control and Disarmament by James E. Dougherty, May 1973 (Out of print)

The Military Indoctrination of Soviet Youth by Leon Goure, January 1973 (Out of print)

The Asian Alliance: Japan and United States Policy by Franz Michael and Gaston J. Sigur, October 1972 (Out of print)

Iran, the Arabian Peninsula, and the Indian Ocean by R.M. Burrell and Alvin J. Cottrell, September 1972 (Out of print)

Soviet Naval Power: Challenge for the 1970s by Norman Polmar, April 1972. Revised edition, September 1974 (Out of print)

How Can We Negotiate with the Communists? by Gerald L. Steibel, March 1972 (Out of print)

Soviet Political Warfare Techniques, Espionage and Propaganda in the 1970s by Lyman B. Kirkpatrick, Jr., and Howland H. Sargeant, January 1972 (Out of print)

The Soviet Presence in the Eastern Mediterranean by Lawrence L. Whetten, September 1971 (Out of print)

The Military Unbalance: Is the U.S. Becoming a Second Class Power? June 1971 (Out of print)

The Future of South Vietnam by Brigadier F. P. Serong, February 1971 (Out of print)

Strategy and National Interests: Reflections for the

Future by Bernard Brodie, January 1971 (Out of print)

The Mekong River: A Challenge in Peaceful Development for Southeast Asia by Eugene R. Black, December 1970 (Out of print)

Problems of Strategy in the Pacific and Indian Oceans by George G. Thomson, October 1970 (Out of print)

Soviet Penetration into the Middle East by Wynfred Joshua, July 1970. Revised edition, October 1971 (Out of print)

Australian Security Policies and Problems by Justus M. van der Kroef, May 1970 (Out of print)

Detente: Dilemma or Disaster? by Gerald L. Steibel, July 1969 (Out of print)

The Prudent Case for Safeguard by William R. Kintner, June 1969 (Out of print)

OTHER PUBLICATIONS

The Fateful Ends and Shades of SALT: Past . . . Present . . . And Yet to Come? by Paul H. Nitze, James E. Dougherty, and Francis X. Kane, March 1979

Strategic Options for the Early Eighties: What Can Be Done? edited by William R. Van Cleave and W. Scott Thompson, February 1979

Arms, Men, and Military Budgets: Issues for Fiscal Year 1979 by Francis P. Hoeber, David B. Kassing, and William Schneider, Jr., February 1978

Arms, Men, and Military Budgets: Issues for Fiscal Year 1978 edited by Francis P. Hoeber and William Schneider, Jr., May 1977

Oil, Divestiture and National Security edited by Frank N. Trager, December 1976

Arms, Men, and Military Budgets: Issues for Fiscal Year 1977 edited by William Schneider, Jr., and Francis P. Hoeber, May 1976

Indian Ocean Naval Limitations, Regional Issues and Global Implications by Alvin J. Cottrell and Walter F. Hahn, April 1976